Oxford International Primary

Science

Student Book

5

W0044040

Deborah Roberts
Terry Hudson

Alan Haigh
Geraldine Shaw

Language consultants:
John McMahon
Liz McMahon

OXFORD

OXFORD
UNIVERSITY PRESS

Great Clarendon Street, Oxford, OX2 6DP, United Kingdom

Oxford University Press is a department of the University of Oxford. It furthers the University's objective of excellence in research, scholarship, and education by publishing worldwide. Oxford is a registered trade mark of Oxford University Press in the UK and in certain other countries.

© Deborah Roberts, Terry Hudson, Alan Haigh and Geraldine Shaw 2021

The moral rights of the authors have been asserted.

First published in 2014

British Library Cataloguing in Publication Data

Data available

ISBN 978-1-382006583

7 9 10 8 6

Paper used in the production of this book is a natural, recyclable product made from wood grown in sustainable forests. The manufacturing process conforms to the environmental regulations of the country of origin.

Printed in China by Golden Cup

Acknowledgements

The publisher and authors would like to thank the following for permission to use photographs and other copyright material:

Cover: Artwork by Blindsalida. **Photos: p10(bl):** PhiveT / Alamy Stock Photo; **p10(br):** Gtranquillity/Shutterstock; **p12:**Bogdan Wankowicz/Shutterstock; **p13(l):** Cultura Creative (RF)/Alamy Stock Photo; **p13(r):** Martin Shields Alamy Stock Photo; **p14(l):** Richard Semik/Fotolia; **p14(m):** Kellis/Shutterstock; **p14(r):** Arvind Balaraman/Shutterstock; **p14-15:**LorraineHudgins/Shutterstock; **p15(br):** yenwen/E+/Getty Images; **p16(tl):** Chris Mattison/ Alamy Stock Photo; **p16(tm):**imageBROKER/Alamy Stock Photo; **p16(tr):** Jacky Parker/Alamy Stock Photo; **p16(bl):** Unique Vision/ Shutterstock; **p16(br):**Scorpp/Shutterstock; **p17:** petographer / Alamy Stock Photo; **p18(t):** Shutterstock; **p18(mr):** Richard Griffin/ Shutterstock**; p18(b):** Michael Flippo/Dreamstime.com; **p18(ml):** ntdanai/Shutterstock; **p19(t):** tom viggars/Alamy Stock Photo; **p19(m):**Dorling Kindersley ltd / Alamy Stock Photo; **p19(b):** Maks Narodenko/Shutterstock; **p20(t):** Fotolia; **p20(b):** Bruce MacQueen/ Shutterstock; **p21:** Dorling Kindersley ltd / Alamy Stock Photo; **p22(bl):** Brian Jackson/Alamy Stock Photo; **p22(br):** Ernie Janes / Alamy Stock Photo; **p23:** Paulo Oliveira/Alamy Stock Photo; **p24:** Charles E Mohr/Science Photo library; **p25(tl):** daniiD/Shutterstock; **p25(tr):** Fiona M. Donnelly/Shutterstock; **p25(bl):** FLPA/Alamy Stock Photo; **p25(br):**muhamad mizan bin ngateni/Shutterstock; **p26(t):** Javier Torrent, VW Pics/Science Photo library; **p26(l):** Linda Burgess/ Photolibrary/Shutterstock; **p26(m):** Andrea Geiss/Shutterstock; **p26(r):** Aravind/Moment Open/Getty Images; **p28:** J. NATAYO/ Shutterstock; **p29:** Pablosdoc/Shutterstock; **p31:** Robert Mertl/ Shutterstock; **p34:** alybaba/Shutterstock; **p36(t):**cheerz/iStockphoto;

p36(bl): Shutterstock; **p36(bm):** Shutterstock; **p36(br):** Mario. bono/Shutterstock; **p37:** Misses Jones/Shutterstock; **p38:** Vanyatko/ Shutterstock; **p40:** Nigel Cattlin/Alamy Stock Photo; **p43:** Cathyrose Melloan/Alamy Stock Photo; **p44(t):** Shutterstock; **p44(b):** ixstudio/ Alamy Stock Photo; **p46(tl):** Global Warming Images/Alamy Stock Photo; **p46(tr):** travellinglight/Alamy Stock Photo; **p46(b):** Diyana Dimitrova/Shutterstock; **p50(tl):** Paul Maguire/Shutterstock; **p50(tml):** Heiko Kiera/Shutterstock; **p50(tmr):** James Laurie/ Shutterstock; **p50(tr):** Rudmer Zwerver/Shutterstock; **p50-51:** robertharding / Alamy Stock Photo; **p51(t):** Steve Bloom Images/ Alamy Stock Photo; **p51(b):** Ian Kenny/Alamy Stock Photo; **p52:** Martin Harvey / Alamy Stock Photo; **p54(tl):** kosam/Shutterstock; **p54(tm):** orxy/Shutterstock; **p54(tr):**Adisa/Shutterstock; **p54(ml):** Vicuschika/Shutterstock; **p54(mr):** Joe Gough/Shutterstock; **p54(b):** Megan R. Hoover/Shutterstock; **p55(tl):** Kitch Bain/Shutterstock; **p55(tml):** Ttstudio/Shutterstock; **p55(m):** Shutterstock; **p55(tmr):** Dirk Ercken/Shutterstock; **p55(tr):** Shutterstock; **p57:** C.K. Lorenz/ Science Photo Library; **p58(t):** Pim Leijen/Shutterstock; **p58(m):** Susanne Masters/Alamy Stock Photo; **p59:** kavram/Shutterstock; **p60(r):** Arto Hakola/Alamy Stock Photo; **p60(l):** Susan Isakson/Alamy Stock Photo; **p62:** Nicky Rhodes/Shutterstock; **p64:** flafabri/Alamy Stock Photo; **p66(tl):** iStockphoto; **p66(tm):**ZouZou/Shutterstock; **p66(tr):** oliveromg/Shutterstock; **p66(bl):** Ron Levine/Digital Vision/ Getty Images; **p66(bm):**StockLite/Shutterstock; **p66(br):** LightField Studios/Shutterstock; **p71(bl):** Cultura Creative/Alamy Stock Photo; **p71(br):**David R. Frazier Photolibrary, Inc./Alamy Stock Photo; **p70-71:** Carsten Reisinger/Shutterstock; **p72:** Oleksiy Mark/Shutterstock; **p74(t):** ngramimagelibrary/foodandbeverage/OUP; **p74(m):** Shaiith/ Shutterstock; **p74(b):** Jochen Tack/Alamy Stock Photo; **p75:** artjazz/ Shutterstock; **p76(l):** Fizkes/Shutterstock; **p76(r):** antoniodiaz/ Shutterstock; p77:Huyangshu/Shutterstock; **p78(l):** Martyn F. Chillmaid/Science Photo Library; **p78(r):** Martyn F. Chillmaid/Science Photo Library; **p85:** Kekyalyaynen/Fotolia; **p88(t):** Sakura Image Inc/ Shutterstock; **p88(b):** ZouZou/Shutterstock; **p90(t):** Andrew Lambert Photography/Science Photo Library; **p90(b):** Peter Righteous / Alamy Stock Photo; **p91:** Anastasia traveller/Alamy Stock Photo; **p94:** Valentin Valkov/Shutterstock; **p95:** Khoroshunova Olga/Shutterstock; **p95(b):** ESA/Hubble/NASA; **p97(r):**Reto Stöckli, Nazmi El Saleous, and Marit Jentoft-Nilsen, NASA GSFC; **p97(l):** Stocktrek Images, Inc./ Alamy Stock Photo; **p99:** Chris Howes/Wild Places Photography / Alamy Stock Photo; **p100:** Pekka Parviainen/Science Photo Library; **p104:**sasimoto/Shutterstock; **p106(l):** Vitalii Matokha/Shutterstock; **p106(r):** gyn9037/Shutterstock; **p108(l):** Smit/Shutterstock; **p108(r):** Smit/Shutterstock; **p110(t):** Wolfgang Kloehr/Shutterstock; **p110(b):** Naci Yavuz/Shutterstock; **p111:** Aleksey Tugolukov/123RF; **p114(b):** Ted Foxx/Alamy Stock Photo; **p114-115:** Shutterstock; **p115(bl):** Mark Cassino/Dembinsky Photo Associates/Alamy Stock Photo; **p115(br):** ifong/Shutterstock; **p117:** Science History Images/Alamy Stock Photo; **p112:**Belinda Pretorius/Dreamstime.com; **p126:** Faraways/Shutterstock; **p127(t):** Graphic design/Shutterstock; **p127(b):**Artography/Shutterstock; **p128:** Khafizov Ivan Harisovich/ Shutterstock; **p130:** Monkey Business Images/Shutterstock; **p131:** Jacek Chabraszewski/Shutterstock; **p136:** Germanskydiver/ Dreamstime.com; **p139:** Thaiways/Alamy Stock Photo; **p140(t):** Ljupco Smokovski/Shutterstock; **p140(ml):** Anton Starikov/ Shutterstock; **p140(mr):** DJTaylor/Shutterstock; **p140(bl):** Rob Walls/ Alamy Stock Photo; **p140(br):** Smileus/Shutterstock; **p149:** G. K./ Shutterstock.

Artwork by Q2A Media Services Pvt. Ltd.

Every effort has been made to contact copyright holders of material reproduced in this book. Any omissions will be rectified in subsequent printings if notice is given to the publisher.

Contents

Contents

How to Use this Book

This Student Book for Oxford International Primary Science forms part of your science lessons for this year. Your teacher will introduce the ideas through whole-class activities, then you will explore them in more detail using this book, before all coming back together to discuss what you have learned. Find out more at: www.oxfordprimary.com/international-science

Structure of the book

This book is divided into five units plus a *Being a Good Scientist* introduction and a picture Glossary:

Being a Good Scientist
Unit 1 Life Cycle and Growth of Flowering Plants
Unit 2 Life Cycles and Growth of Animals and Humans
Unit 3 Properties and Changes of Materials
Unit 4 Earth and Space
Unit 5 Forces in Action
Glossary

Each unit covers a different strand of science. You will need a science notebook to write in and to record your investigation results and conclusions.

Being a good scientist

To be a good scientist you need to be curious and ask questions. This section will help you think about how to develop your scientific skills to work like a scientist.

What you will find in each unit

There are three types of lessons:
Wow introduces each unit's scientific ideas and key words. It tells you what you will learn in the unit and lets you discuss what you already know.
Focused lessons cover the scientific knowledge and skills you need to learn this year.
In **What have I learned?** you review your learning and show your teacher what you have learned about the unit.

What you will find in the lessons

Although each lesson is unique, they have common features:

The words on the Wow pages are included in the picture glossary at the back of the book. You can add your own notes for each word.

Key words Gives you the key words for the lesson.

In this lesson you will explore the life cycle of an insect. Tells you what you will learn in the lesson.

Questions to help you talk to each other and share ideas about the science you are learning and the investigations you do.

Practical and research activities to investigate and report on science topics. Sometimes your teacher will ask you to use different equipment, which is available in school. They may also ask you to carry out a test in a different way, to make sure you are safe.

Stretch zone Challenges you to take your learning further.

Key idea Summarises what you have learned.

Additional features

Think back Reminds you what has been covered before.

Science fact Interesting and amazing science facts.

Highlights the skills needed to be a good scientist.

Important notes about how to stay safe.

Teacher's Guide

There is a Teacher's Guide to help your teacher to work out the resources needed and to offer alternative activities and approaches.

Workbook

At the bottom of each page in this book is a link to a Workbook, where you can record your work and get extra practice to do in your lesson or at home.

Being a Good Scientist

Science is the study of the world around us. To be a good scientist you need to be curious and ask questions. This section will help you think about how to build on your scientific skills to plan and carry out more complicated investigations.

Your work as a scientist this year will allow you to develop further your scientific skills. You will make more detailed predictions and observe patterns in your results. Having detected patterns in data, you will need to decide if these are the result of your investigation or simply happened by chance. You will also need to decide if your results were accurate and valid. You will have to think more deeply about how living and non-living things are classified. You will also be expected to test your own ideas and use scientific evidence.

This diagram shows the steps you can take to plan and carry out investigations like a scientist.

Start here:
Asking questions

- Exploring ideas and thinking of questions to investigate.

Making a prediction

- What do I already know that will help me to decide what is likely to happen?

Planning

- Which is the best type of test to carry out?
- What are the variables?
- Which need to be controlled and why?
- How can I find out more before I start?
- Which secondary sources shall I use?
- What equipment do I need?

Presenting ideas

- Have I used scientific language and illustrations?
- Should I present my ideas by speaking, by writing or by using displays and computer presentations? Would a model help?
- Does my work lead to other questions to study?

Recording findings

- What is the best way to record data?
- Should I present the data in tables, scatter graphs, bar graphs or line graphs?
- Should I use scientific diagrams and labels?
- Is a classification key useful?
- Can I record into a table?
- Would photographs or film be helpful?
- Would a written description work well?

Making observations

- What observations and measurements should I make?
- How long should I make observations and measurements for?
- When do I repeat measurements?
- What equipment should I use?

Drawing conclusions

- Does the data show that the research question has been answered?
- Are further tests needed?
- Does the evidence support my ideas?
- Do I trust my results?
- How can I improve the investigation?

Asking questions

You have been encouraged to start your investigation questions with words such as 'which', 'what', 'why', 'how', 'do' and 'does'. This can help to lead you towards planning an investigation or carrying out research that will have a clear answer. The better you are at forming a question, the easier you will find it to plan and carry out investigations. Different types of questions are used in different situations.

Finding out what is happening: verification questions

These questions are designed to help you to collect data to find something out about a situation. You don't need to know anything about it before your investigation. For example:

- Is it raining today?
- Do bees fly at night?
- Does salt dissolve in water?

Answers to these questions will help you to build your knowledge, and the questions will lead you towards the type of investigation to carry out.

Select one of the questions. Talk about what type of investigation you could carry out to answer the question.

Finding out why things happen: theory questions

These questions need you to have some prior knowledge of the subject. The question also means you have to explain WHY something happened. For example:

- Why does a large parachute fall through the air slower than a small parachute?
- Why do seeds need soil and water in order to germinate?

Should we stir it or not? How much salt should we add?

Experimental questions

These are the questions you will be asking and trying to answer when you plan and carry out investigations. These questions grow from your prior knowledge of the topic; they need an explanation and they are testable. In other words, other people can test your answer to see if they agree. For example:

- Does more salt dissolve in warm water than in cold water?
- Are pollinating insects attracted to one colour of petal more than others?

Read the three questions below. Decide whether they are verification, theory or experimental questions. Talk about how you would plan to answer the questions.

1 What time will the Sun rise tomorrow?
2 If salt is added to water, does it freeze at a different temperature?
3 Why do green plants need sunlight?

Making a prediction

When answering a research or investigation question you should make a prediction.

This is based on what you already know about a topic. Scientists are usually confident about what will happen in an investigation. They may have done similar investigations before or read about similar work elsewhere.

Use what you know about forces to help you think about this question.

> What would you observe if you dropped a light and a heavy object into soft sand?

As a scientist, you draw on your previous experiences to help. You think about when you have seen objects falling. This makes your prediction much better than a guess. It is based on scientific knowledge and evidence.

Scientists may use **models** and **diagrams** to represent objects and systems. These help scientists explain and think about scientific ideas that are not visible or unknown. Scientists can then use their models and diagrams to make predictions or to explain observations.

Remember: a prediction can be shown to be incorrect. An investigation, no matter how often it is repeated, may show that your original prediction cannot be the correct answer.

> What would you do if your prediction is shown by your investigation to be incorrect?

Planning

It is vital that scientists plan what they are going to do. They discuss their plan to check it will work. A good scientist will also research the topic to find out as much as they can. They use secondary sources.

A secondary source is any source that gives you information you have not found out for yourself. Examples are written information in books and on the internet, talks from people who did the original work, documentaries, journals, magazines or newspapers.

Use secondary sources when you can but be careful. Some can be trusted more than others. A science textbook or science article in a journal has been checked by other scientists to see that the information is accurate and up to date. Other sources may not be accurate or may even be totally wrong. Try to use more than one source of information and check it by doing investigations yourself when you can.

Remember: scientists think carefully about the equipment they will need. They make a list and make sure everything is available before they start an investigation.

Different types of test

Descriptive investigations

This is when you observe something over time and describe what happens, for example, collecting and observing caterpillars over time to observe the life cycle of butterflies. You do not need to know anything about the topic and you do not need a prediction. You are recording what you see and then making sense of it.

Discuss a descriptive test you have carried out. What were you observing? Which scientific skills were you using? How did you record and present your findings?

Comparative investigations

This is when you compare different things. For example, which material soaks up water better or which type of shoe grips the most on a surface? In a comparative investigation you report about similarities and differences.

You will be encouraged to set up what are called comparative tests. This is when you design an investigation to compare different things. For example, you could compare the strengths of different magnets.

Experimental investigations

This is when you will be designing a fair test. This means you will have to decide on which factor or variable you will alter, which you will measure, and which you will control. The investigation is set up to gather data that supports or does not support a causal relationship. This means we are investigating if changing X causes or makes Y change.

The types of variable are described below:

- **Independent variable** (sometimes called the manipulative variable) – this is what you change on purpose in an investigation.

- **Dependent variable** (sometimes called the response variable) – this is what changes during the investigation because you have altered the independent variable. It is what you measure.

- **Control variables** (sometimes called constants) – these are the variables you keep the same during an investigation.

Study the picture. Discuss and identify the independent, dependent and control variables for this investigation. What causal effect are the students studying? What would your prediction be?

Surveys of habitats also need to be fair. You should survey the same amount of ground so you can do a fair comparison with other areas. This is why quadrats are so important: they make it easier to sample the same amount of ground in different areas.

Science fact

Scientists sometimes give a suggested answer to an investigation. This is called a hypothesis. If other scientists test this and they all agree, it then becomes a theory. In time, a theory that does not change can become a law of science.

Sometimes it is not possible to plan an investigation to answer your questions. For example, if you want to explore forces that are too strong for you to investigate, you cannot carry out a test. In this case you can use secondary sources.

What are secondary sources? List the times you have used them to find out about a topic.

Making observations

Scientists use their observation skills during investigations.

> What observations and measurements would the students investigating the ramps on page 9 be carrying out? Make a list.

During the planning stage you will decide which observations and measurements you need to make. This will depend on the type of investigation you are carrying out.

With surveys, this may involve counting different living things and observing what they look like to help with identification.

With experimental investigations, this can involve measuring the time taken for something to happen, the height that something has grown, the temperature of a material, or the number of grams of something.

Scientists also decide the best place to carry out observations. They think about the equipment they need, the safety measures that need to be followed, and the reason for the investigation. For example, a survey of animals in a habitat is carried out in a particular outdoor location and a chemistry experiment is usually carried out in a laboratory.

Scientists use devices such as computers, data loggers and other devices, such as smartphones and electronic scales, to help them to take accurate measurements.

Science fact

Scientists use standard units to record their results. These units have been agreed throughout the world so all scientists can compare their work. The standard unit for length is the metre or kilometre.

Good scientists repeat measurements. This is to make sure they have not made any mistakes. They can then calculate a mean average for their readings. The example below shows the results of a ramp investigation.

> Which standard units would you use to measure: a) temperature, b) distance between villages, c) the amount of flour needed in a recipe?

Angle of ramp (degrees)	Time taken for a ball to roll down the ramp (seconds)			
	count 1	count 2	count 3	mean average
10	8	7	9	
30	5	4	6	
50	4	2	3	

> What is the average reading for each angle of ramp? Which slope allowed the ball to roll down the quickest? Why is it useful to not just take the first readings?

Remember: in some investigations you may use a key to help you to identify living things and objects.

Recording findings

As part of the planning process, scientists think about the best way to record their results. They might decide to use a table or labelled diagrams. They could take photographs or film what is happening. The main thing to think about is:

> How can I record results so they help me to see patterns or to sort things into groups?

You will need to use your results to draw conclusions. This is the next part of the investigation process. If you do not record your results carefully, you may not be able to make the most sensible conclusions.

Tables

You will often record your results in a table.

water | no water

> Design a table to compare the height change of a seedling grown with water and another seedling of the same type of plant grown without water over 6 days.

Stretch zone

List the independent, dependent and control variables for a well-planned investigation which looks at the effects of watering on seedling growth.

Charts/graphs

You have presented your results as bar and line charts or graphs, like the ones below.

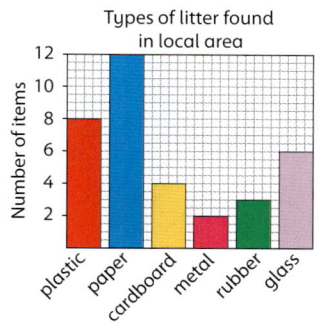

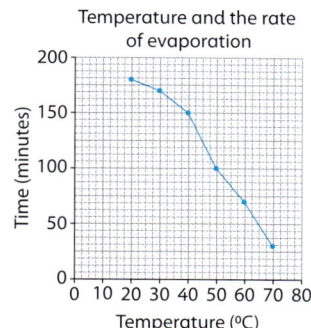

A bar chart is used when there are separate categories or types of things being studied. These are on the horizontal axis as separate bars.

A line graph is used to plot individual points where the values on the horizontal axis and vertical axis are both numbers. The points are joined together to make a continuous line. These graphs are used to show a trend.

A scatter graph is like a line graph but the points do not show a simple relationship. Instead, they are not joined up but still show a pattern or trend.

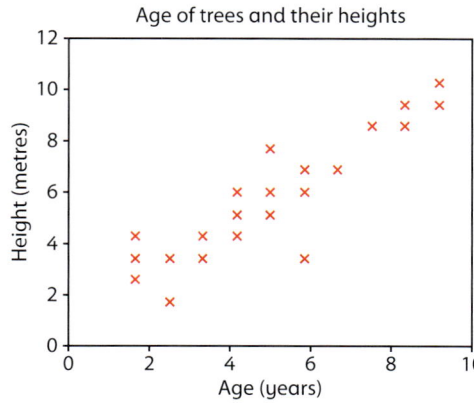

The height of the trees is plotted on the y-axis. The ages of the trees are plotted on the x-axis.

> Why is the scatter graph better here than a bar graph or line graph? What is the relationship between the age of a tree and its height?

Drawings, photographs and videos

You have worked with scientific drawings before. Remember they are not like the pictures you paint. Scientific drawings are much simpler.

Scientists also use modern technology to take photographs and video clips of their investigations and results.

Photographs show a lot of detail

This is a very accurate way to record results. This level of detail would not be possible without using a camera.

Filming allows us to see things that may be impossible to see in person. Scientists can observe what happens to a germinating seed and time the details accurately by slowing down a film and piecing it together. This is called time-lapsed filming.

Research time-lapse films of germinating seeds on the internet. Choose the best one to share with your class. What does the film show that you could not see with drawings or photos?

Drawing conclusions

The last stage of an investigation is when scientists look at their results carefully. It is at this stage that they make sense of their results. They work out if the results have helped them to answer their investigation question.

The questions they might ask are:

Can I *see* any patterns?

Is there a causal relationship in the data: did one thing cause another thing to happen?

Are any results unusual? Should I repeat any parts of the investigation?

Was my prediction correct? Does the evidence support my ideas?

How much do I trust the results?

Do secondary sources of information support my ideas?

Are further tests needed?

Scientists also link their conclusions to bigger scientific ideas. For example, if they are thinking about objects falling through the air, they will link this to their knowledge of gravity and surface area. They will also think about other factors, such as how heavy an object is and what its shape is, and they will even think about wider examples such as the shape of seeds and bird wings. They may even consider inventions such as helicopters and aeroplanes.

After completing an investigation, a good scientist will study their results and think about what went well and what could be improved. This is called evaluation and is an important part of the investigation process.

Presenting ideas

Scientists present their ideas by talking to others informally or at more formal meetings and conferences. They also write reports or make displays. This might be in a poster or computer presentation. They may include models.

Scientists are very careful to use the correct scientific language. This makes their ideas much clearer. They use standard units so their findings make sense across the world. They also plan their reports and presentations to match the audience. For example, if they are talking to people who are not scientists, they will not include as much detail as they would in a more formal scientific paper.

Tips for presenting ideas

- Plan on paper first.
- Discuss your work with your team and share out the jobs.
- Think about your audience.
- Do not put too much information on a slide, poster or web page.
- Make any text, pictures and models eye-catching and clear.
- Use headings, colour and lists.
- Clearly set out what you did and what you found out.
- Show how your work leads onto further work.
- Use secondary sources of information and give credit to the people whose work you are using.
- Practise your presentation.
- Enjoy sharing ideas.

It is useful to fill out an investigation planning form. This sets out all the stages of your investigation. It helps you to remember everything you need to think about. Your teacher can give you one of these.

1 Life Cycle and Growth of Flowering Plants

In this unit you will:

- explore that plants reproduce
- observe the structure of flowering plants
- describe the life cycle of flowering plants
- find out about the processes of pollination, fertilisation, seed production, seed dispersal and germination
- investigate the conditions seeds need to germinate
- explore the conditions plants need to grow well.

energy   fertilisation   fruit   germination   growth   life cycle   pollination   reproduction   seed dispersal   warmth   water

Discuss the different stages A to C of the plant in the photographs.

Do you know what happens between stages C and A?

What does the plant need to help it to grow?

Why do you think insects, such as butterflies, are so important to flowering plants?

Science fact

The largest trees in the world are the Giant Redwoods. They grow to a height of over 100 metres and can have a circumference of 20 metres!

■ For more activities, go to Workbook 5 pages 14–15.

The structure of flowering plants

In this lesson you will explore the structure of flowering plants.

Key words

flower

fruit

leaves

root

seeds

stem (trunk)

Think back

Plants can be classified into two groups called flowering plants and non-flowering plants.

moss

fern leaves

conifer cones

Mosses, ferns and conifer trees are examples of non-flowering plants. Most non-flowering plants do not produce seeds. They make spores. Conifer trees do produce seeds but these are found in hard cones. Mosses do not have roots. They grow on top of soil, bark or rocks and they take in water through their leaves.

Science fact

Bamboo flowers are very rare. The bamboo plants may only produce flowers after 65 years, or even 120 years!

Some plants and trees produce flowers. These are flowering plants.

We use flowering plants for many things. They can make local areas very beautiful. They can also be used for foods and to provide medicines.

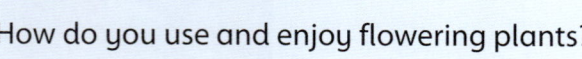

Talk about any flowering plants you have observed and investigated.

How do you use and enjoy flowering plants?

■ For more activities, go to Workbook 5 page 16.

Parts of a flowering plant

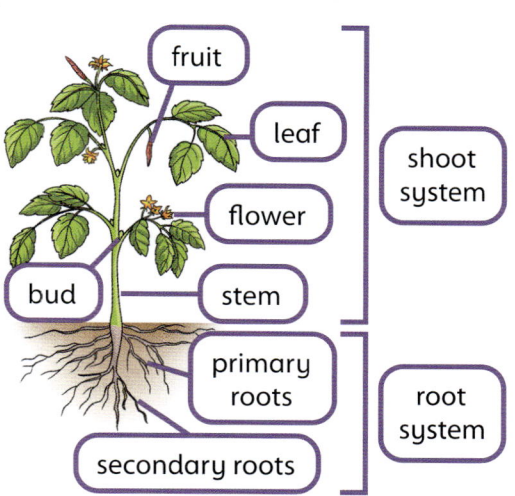

fruit

leaf

flower

bud

stem

shoot system

primary roots

secondary roots

root system

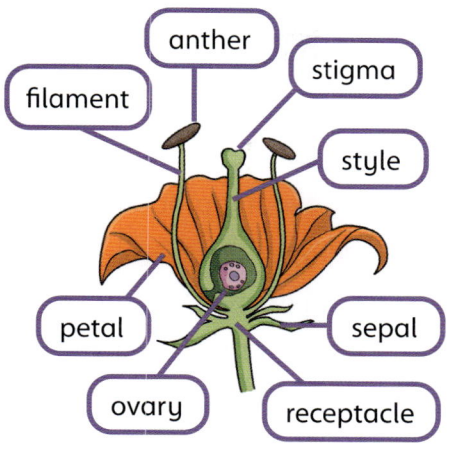

anther

filament

stigma

style

petal

sepal

ovary

receptacle

Look at the diagrams of the flowering plant.

Talk about which parts of the plant you have seen before.

Agree on the function of each part of the plant.

Identifying the parts of a flowering plant

You will be given a flowering plant to study.

1 Carefully remove the plant from the pot. Wash the roots carefully with tap water and dry them with a paper towel.

2 Spread your plant out on a paper sheet. Stick it in place and then label all of the parts.

3 Place a paper sheet over the plant and cover this with a piece of cardboard.

4 Add books or other heavy objects on top of the cardboard.

5 Leave your flower in a safe place for a few days.

6 Remove the books, cardboard and covering paper. Display your flattened plant on a wall as a poster.

Compare all of the plant posters in your classroom.

How are the plants the same?

How are they different?

Stretch zone

Identify a non-flowering plant in your area. Get permission before taking a small sample. Press and display it as you did for the flowering plant. Label some of the differences between the non-flowering plant and the flowering plant.

Key idea

Flowering plants have common parts.

■ For more activities, go to Workbook 5 page 17.

Flowering plants and reproduction

In this lesson you will learn that plants produce offspring through reproduction.

Plants make new versions of themselves through reproduction. Many plants do this by producing spores, buds or new parts of their roots. This method makes identical copies of the plant. They all have the same characteristics. This is called asexual reproduction.

Flowering plants reproduce by making seeds. Seeds often form by pollen from one plant combining with an ovule of another. This gives a chance for characteristics from both plants to be mixed. This method of reproduction is called sexual reproduction.

We call this process the life 'cycle' because each stage is repeated each time a new plant is made. There are four main stages in the life cycle of a flowering plant:

❶ Seeds

We can think of seeds as the first stage in the life cycle of flowering plants. Seeds need to have the right conditions, such as water and warmth, to start to grow. Once a seed starts to grow we say it has germinated.

❷ Seedlings

We can think of seedlings as the second stage in the life cycle. We start to see the first shoots and roots at this stage.

shoots

roots

❹ Adult plants

We can think of adult plants as the fourth stage in the life cycle. At this stage the plant is fully grown.

❸ Young plants

We can think of young plants as the third stage in the life cycle. At this stage we should be able to identify what kind of plant it is.

Think back to your earlier work on flowering plants. Their life cycle from seeds to adult plants will be explored in the following lessons.

■ For more activities, go to Workbook 5 page 18.

How do flowering plants reproduce?

Your teacher will give you a flowering plant.

1. Carefully remove a flower and a leaf. Cut some small pieces off the stem and roots. Collect some seeds.

2. Plant the flower in a small plant pot full of compost or soil. Add a small amount of water and place the pot in a warm place.

3. Do the same for each of the plant parts you have collected.

4. Check your pots every day and keep the compost damp.

5. Record when you see any seedlings appear.

6. Create a poster to show how you did your investigation. Include drawings and your conclusions.

Did the seedlings grow from the flower, the leaf, the stem, the seeds or the root?

Be a scientist

Researchers often present their results as a poster at conferences. This allows them to share their findings with others.
▶ page 13

▶ page 13

Science fact

Some new plants can be formed from taking cuttings of parts of the plant, but the main way flowering plants reproduce is through seeds.

Stretch zone

Use the internet or books to produce a short report about the reproduction of watermelon plants. Answer these questions.

1. The watermelon plant hides its seeds inside a fleshy fruit that is good to eat. Why?

2. What happens to the seeds when animals eat the fruit?

3. Why does the watermelon produce 600 seeds, not six seeds?

Key idea

Flowering plants reproduce in a cycle. They start as a seed and grow into adult plants, which then produce more seeds.

19

■ For more activities, go to Workbook 5 page 19.

Observing seeds

In this lesson you will examine the structure of seeds and observe seeds as they start to grow.

Key words
cotyledon
embryo
seed

Seeds have a strong seed coat to protect them. Each seed contains an embryo. The embryo will grow into the new plant by producing shoots and roots.

Seeds also have a food store called a cotyledon. Some seeds have one cotyledon and others have two.

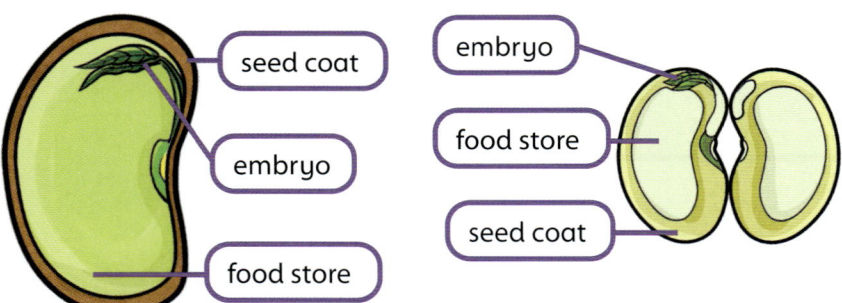

seed coat

embryo

food store

embryo

food store

seed coat

Study the diagrams of the seeds.

Which has one cotyledon and which has two?

Talk about why a seed would need a food store and an embryo.

Science fact

Many seeds are so tough they can pass all the way through an animal's digestive system without being damaged.

■ For more activities, go to Workbook 5 page 20.

Investigating how seeds grow

Scientists believe that no matter which way up a seed is planted, the roots will always grow downwards and the shoots will always grow upwards. You can test this.

1   Use bean seeds and grow them in the way shown in the photograph.

2   Add a small amount of water to a jar and swirl it round. Fold kitchen paper and pack it into the jar. Add some water so the kitchen paper is damp.

3   Place your seeds into your jar so they are trapped between the paper and the glass. Put a lid on the jar.

4   Add a small amount of water to the seeds every few days.

5   Observe what happens to the seeds. Every two days turn the jars over. Draw the seeds every time you turn the jar.

6   Which direction did the shoots and roots grow? Did they change direction after you turned the jar? Write a report to share your findings.

Stretch zone

Find out how the shoots and roots 'know' the correct direction for them to grow. Present your findings to the class.

Key ideas

- Seeds contain an embryo to make a new plant, and food stores for the growing plant.

- When a seed starts to grow (germinate) the shoots grow upwards and the roots grow downwards.

1 Life Cycle and Growth of Flowering Plants

■ For more activities, go to Workbook 5 page 21.

Spreading seeds by wind and water

In this lesson you will learn how seeds are dispersed by wind and water.

Key words

germinate

seed dispersal

variable

Think back

Can you remember why it is important that seeds are spread out away from the parent plant?

What happens to the seeds?

Seeds move away from where they are made. When seeds have been spread out, we say they have been dispersed.

Not every seed can find somewhere to grow into a new plant and so not all seeds germinate. Plants produce a lot of seeds so that some of them will find a place to grow.

There are four main ways that seeds are dispersed:

- by wind
- by water
- by 'explosion'
- by animals.

In this lesson, you will explore the first two ways – wind and water. In the next lesson, you will explore the others.

Wind

Usually these seeds are very light and can be blown by the wind.

Some seeds have 'wings' or 'parachute' structures. This helps them to stay in the air longer. They can then travel further.

Look at the seeds in the photographs. How is their shape helping them to be dispersed?

■ For more activities, go to Workbook 5 page 22.

Spreading seeds by wind

You are going to design a model seed that takes a long time to fall through the air.

Design your shape from one piece of A4 paper. Use all of the paper. The paper can be cut, folded or glued.

1 Build your seed.

2 Test it by timing how long it takes to fall.

3 Repeat the test three times. You will need to start all of the seeds from the same height to control the variables.

4 Record the times in a table. Work out the mean (average) time by adding the three times together and dividing by three.

Be a scientist

A variable is the thing that can change. Scientists keep all variables in an investigation the same, apart from the variable being measured.

▶ page 9

Compare your model seeds with others in the class.

Which shapes took the longest time to fall?

Water

Some plants that live in or near water, such as a river or the sea, can use the water to help them disperse their seeds. Seeds can travel a long way on water.

When seeds have been dispersed, they start to grow. We already know that seeds need the right conditions, like water and warmth, to help them to germinate.

A coconut starting to grow

Talk about how water has helped this large seed to travel.

What might happen if this seed landed near the parent plant?

Stretch zone

Use the internet or books to research more examples of plants that disperse their seeds by wind and by water. How do the seeds look different? Produce a presentation to share your research.

Key idea

Seeds can be dispersed from the parent plant by wind or water to find a place to grow.

■ For more activities, go to Workbook 5 page 23.

Spreading seeds by animals and explosion

In this lesson you will learn how seeds are dispersed by animals and explosion.

Key words
adapted
animal
explosion
germinate
seed dispersal

Think back

The purpose of seeds is to germinate and grow into new plants in good conditions. This is why they need to be dispersed. List the two methods of seed dispersal that you have already learned about.

You have already seen that seeds come in a wide range of shapes and sizes. Seeds have adapted to get a long way away from the parent plant. Let's look at some more of these adaptations, this time of seeds that are dispersed by 'explosion' or by animals.

Explosion

Some plants can disperse seeds through explosions. Their seed pods actually shoot the seeds out, sometimes quite a long way. The seeds can then grow into new flowering plants.

Seed explosion

Building an exploding seed pod

You can build your own exploding seed pod using small, smooth seeds and a balloon.

1 Stretch the balloon gently.

2 Use a funnel to put some seeds inside the balloon.

3 Blow the balloon up and tie off the end.

  You now have your seed pod.

4 Go outside and spread out a cloth or large piece of paper.

  Stand at the end of the cloth or paper.

5 Hold the balloon at arm's length and burst the balloon with a sharp pencil.

6 Observe what happens. Measure how far the seeds spread.

7 Write a report of your investigation.

  Include an explanation about why this method is so useful to plants.

 **Warning!**
Be careful when blowing into the balloon. Make sure you don't suck up any seeds!

■ For more activities, go to Workbook 5 page 24.

Animals

Seeds can be carried a long way by animals and birds, and even by people!

Some seeds can stick to fur or clothes and be transported far away. They are then brushed off or drop off at a new location.

Some seeds are eaten and then pass through the animal unharmed to be deposited at a new location.

Some seeds are buried for food by animals or birds, and then forgotten about.

How does having a tough seed coat help seeds to be dispersed?

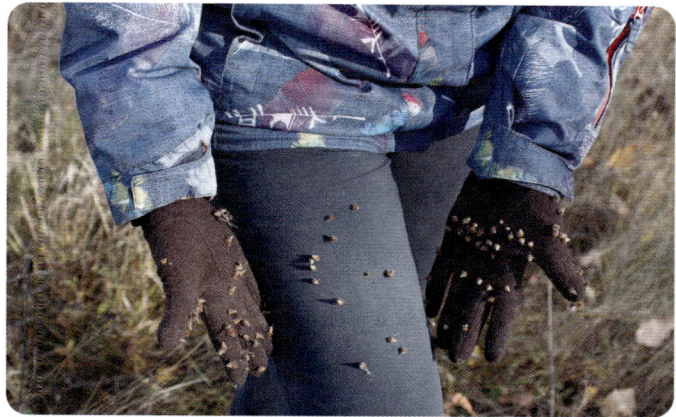

Science fact

The spiky or hooked cases around some seeds are called burrs. They can stick to fur, feathers and even clothes.

 Stretch zone

Design an investigation to show which types of seeds stick the best to fur. Discuss the design with a partner to evaluate it.

Key idea

Seeds can be dispersed from the parent plant by explosion or animals to find a place to grow.

■ For more activities, go to Workbook 5 page 25.

Pollinating flowers

In this lesson you will learn about pollination.

Key words
insect
pollen
pollination

Look closely at the photograph. What is the insect doing?

Why are insects attracted to plants?

Some flowering plants need help from insects to produce seeds. When insects move between flowers they are helping the plant to produce seeds.

If you look very closely, you can see that the insect has small particles on its body. These particles are called pollen.

Pollen is very important because it is used by the plant to make seeds. As the insect flies or moves from plant to plant, pollen from one plant sticks to the insect and is dropped on to another plant. When insects drop pollen from one plant on to another plant of the *same* kind, we call this pollination. We say that the insect pollinates the plant.

Some flowering plants produce very sweet liquid called nectar. Nectar provides food for many insects. The plant produces food for the insect and the insect pollinates the plant.

Are there other ways to pollinate plants?

We now know that insects have a big role to play in pollinating plants, but they are not alone! Plants can be pollinated in other ways too.

Why do humans want to pollinate plants?

Plants can be pollinated by humans

Pollen can travel on water to other plants

Birds can help to pollinate plants

■ For more activities, go to Workbook 5 page 26.

The wind and pollen

If you know anyone who suffers from hay fever you will know that pollen can blow around in the air.

Some plants make use of this and are pollinated by this wind-blown pollen.

Plants that use the wind for pollination have open flowers. This is so they are open to the air. Plants that use insect pollination often have tube-like flowers to attract the insects inside.

Study the flowers in the diagrams below.

Which is wind pollinated? Which is insect pollinated?

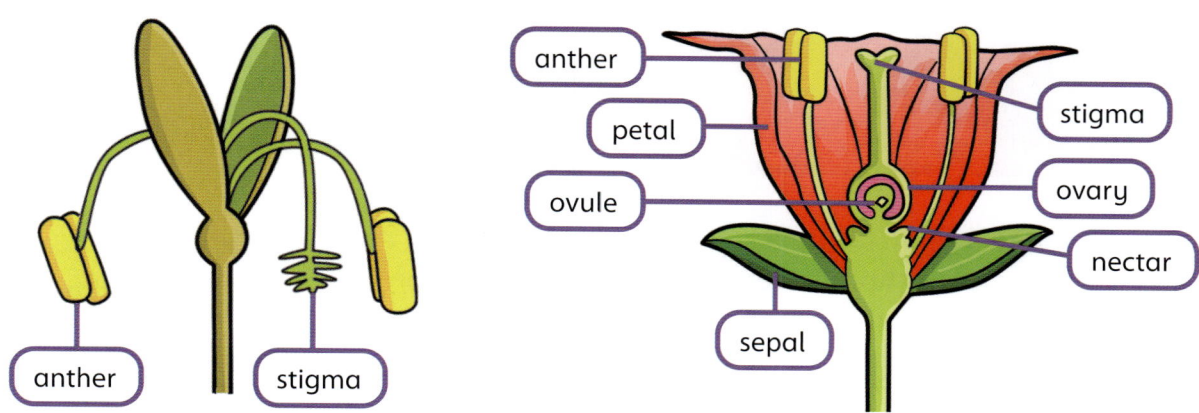

anther

stigma

anther

petal

ovule

stigma

ovary

nectar

sepal

Flower survey

You will carry out a survey of flowers in the school grounds or a local park.

1 Observe the different types of flowers.

2 Find examples that you think are pollinated by insects or other animals.

3 Find examples of flowers that are pollinated by the wind.

4 Draw or photograph one example of each.

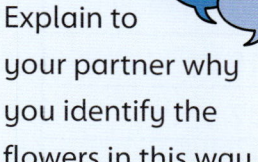

Explain to your partner why you identify the flowers in this way.

5 Make an information leaflet about pollination using findings from your survey.

Stretch zone

Research and tell your partner why wind-pollinated flowers often have anthers and stigma sticking above the flower.

Key idea

Flowering plants need to be pollinated so they can produce seeds.

■ For more activities, go to Workbook 5 page 27.

Attracting insect pollinators

In this lesson you will explore how plants attract insects as pollinators.

Key words

nectar

petal

There are many different shapes and colours of flowers. Many of these shapes and colours are to help the flower attract insects and other animals.

Petal colour

Scientists have investigated how flowers attract insects and other pollinators. First, they studied the colour of the petals.

They used artificial flowers to find out if bees preferred one petal colour to another.

To make it a fair test they made sure the petals were the same size and that observations were made at the same time of the day.

The scientists placed the flowers near lots of bees and counted how many times the bees visited the flowers. Here is a snapshot of their results.

Talk about the investigation. If you were planning it, what would you keep the same (control variable), what would you change (independent variable) and what would you measure or count (dependent variable)?

Petal colour	Number of visits by bees
blue	46
red	15
white	32
yellow	28

The scientists started to draw a bar chart of the information.

 Analysing results about pollinators

1   Draw a bar chart of the results.

2   What do the results tell you about bees and the colour of petals?

■ For more activities, go to Workbook 5 page 28.

Nectar

Flowers also provide a sticky, sugary liquid called nectar to attract insects. The insects drink it or collect it for the colony.

 Does nectar attract more insects?

Plan an investigation to see if artificial flowers with nectar attract more insects than artificial flowers without nectar.

For nectar you can use sugary water or honey mixed with some water.

1   Design and make some flowers. Use one of the colours from the scientists' study on the previous page.

2   Add your nectar to some of the flowers. Leave some of the flowers without nectar. Make sure you know which is which.

3   Leave the flowers outside. Observe them to see which attract the most insects: those with or those without nectar.

4   Record your observations in a table. Present your information as a bar chart.

5   What is your conclusion? Did the flowers with nectar attract more insects?

 Be a scientist

Scientists use the conclusion to answer the question in the title of an investigation.
▶ page 12

Stretch zone

Plan how you could find out if scents attract insects such as bees. Share your ideas with others in the class.

 Science fact

A bat found in Ecuador has a very long tongue that it uses to sip nectar from the bottom of long flowers. The plant benefits as the bats take pollen from flower to flower.

Key idea

Flowers are adapted to attract insects to help pollination.

■ For more activities, go to Workbook 5 page 29.

Looking at flowers in detail

In this lesson you will learn that plants produce flowers which have male and female parts.

Think back

Look at the diagram of the flowering plant on page 17. What parts of the plant below are labelled 1, 2, 3 and 4?

Key words

anther
carpel
filament
ovary
stamen
stigma
style

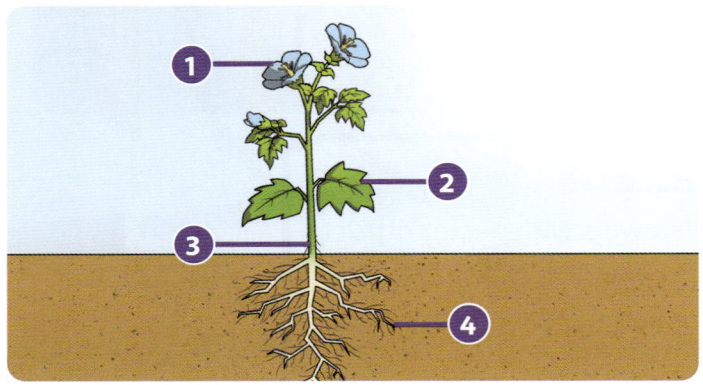

Why is each part of the plant important?

Let's look at a flower in more detail. In a flower there are male and female parts.

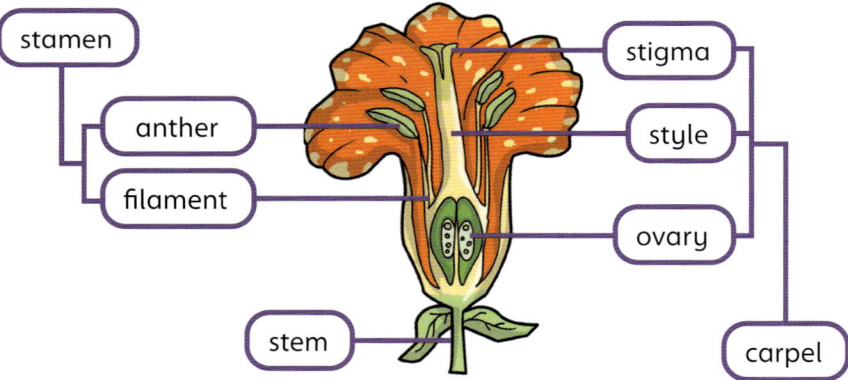

The stamen

The stamen is the male part of the flower and is made up of the filament and the anther. The filament holds the anther in place and the anther is where the pollen is produced.

The carpel

The carpel is the female part of the flower and is made up of the stigma, the style and the ovary. The stigma is very sticky. This helps it to catch pollen. The style holds the stigma in place and the ovary is where the seeds are made. The carpel is sometimes called the pistil.

■ For more activities, go to Workbook 5 page 30.

Identifying the parts of a flower

You have been given a flower. Observe the parts of the flower. Use a hand lens.

1 Draw the whole flower and label the parts.

2 Use tweezers to remove the petals. Stick them to another piece of paper and label them.

3 Then remove the stamens and do the same.

4 Remove the carpel. Carefully cut open the ovary. Stick the carpel onto the paper.

5 Labels the parts. Add a note to explain the function of each part.

6 Display your picture of the flower and your labelled flower parts.

Walk around and study all of the different flowers on display.

How are they the same? How are they different?

Be a scientist

Scientists use instruments to take apart living things to find out more about them. This is called dissection.

▶ page 9

Warning!

Take care with sharp instruments. Do not carry them around the room and keep your fingers clear of the sharp blades.

Stretch zone

Find out how the petals, stamen and carpels differ in wind-pollinated and insect-pollinated flowers. Draw an example of each.

Some plants have separate male and female flowers. A male flower only has a stamen. A female flower only has carpels. An example is the Alder tree. This has long catkins made of only male flowers, but it also has groups of female flowers on the same tree.

Science fact

About 6% of plants make male and female flowers. The rest have flowers that have both male and female parts.

Key idea

Flowers have male and female parts. These different parts produce seeds.

Alder tree catkins

■ For more activities, go to Workbook 5 page 31.

Fertilisation in flowering plants

In this lesson you will learn that seeds are formed when pollen from the male part fertilises the ovule (the female part).

Key words

fertilisation
ovule
pollen nucleus
seed production

Think back

How is pollen moved from one flower to another?

You have learned that pollination is when the pollen from one plant drops onto another plant of the same kind. If we look in more detail, we find that pollen made in the male anther is moved on to the sticky stigma of the female carpel.

Look closely at the diagram below. You can see that the pollen from the male anther is being dropped on to the sticky female stigma of the *same* plant.

stigma · style · anther with pollen · filament · ovary

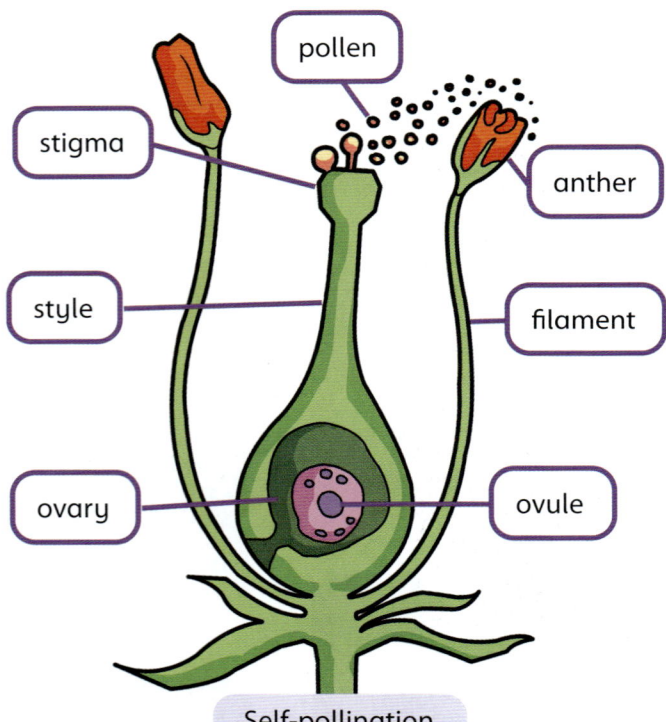

stigma · pollen · anther · style · filament · ovary · ovule

Self-pollination

Why is it useful that the stigma is sticky?

In self-pollination there is less chance of new characteristics being passed onto the next generation of plants when seeds are made. It is better for plants to have pollen from a *different* plant of the same type. This is called cross-pollination.

Talk about how cross-pollination and self-pollination are different. Draw a diagram to show cross-pollination.

32

■ For more activities, go to Workbook 5 page 32.

The flower may be pollinated in lots of different ways, but the next step is always the same.

Look closely at the diagram. Can you see the pollen at the top of the stigma?

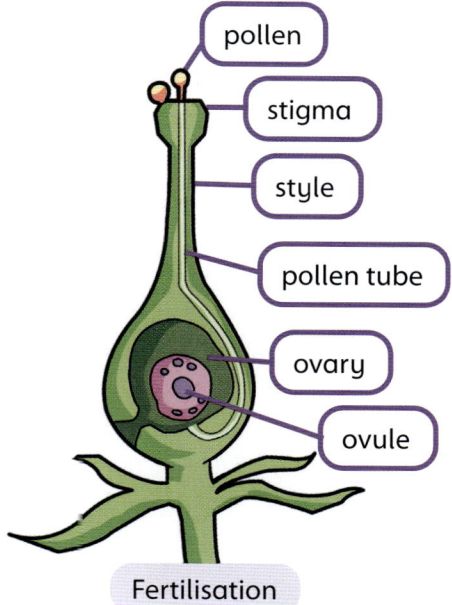

pollen
stigma
style
pollen tube
ovary
ovule

Fertilisation

Science fact

Although most pollen does not travel far, some pollen has been shown to blow over 2000 kilometres in the wind.

Pollen attaches to the sticky stigma. The pollen then sends a pollen tube down the female style. The pollen tube allows part of the pollen called the pollen nucleus to move down inside the style.

The pollen tube connects with the ovary and the pollen nucleus enters the ovary. When the pollen nucleus meets the ovule they join together.

This joining is called fertilisation. This is how a seed is made.

Making a model of fertilisation

You are going to make a model to show how seeds form. Use the materials you have been given.

1 Design your model. It must show:
   • how pollen lands on the female part of the flower
   • how the pollen nucleus gets to the ovary
   • the pollen nucleus joining with the ovule.
2 Build the model.
3 Present your model to the class and explain each stage. Ask for feedback so you can improve it.

Key ideas

• Pollen from one plant joins with an ovule in the ovary of the same or another plant to make a seed.
• The joining is called fertilisation.

■ For more activities, go to Workbook 5 page 33.

Life cycle of flowering plants

In this lesson you will explore that flowering plants have a life cycle.

Key words

fertilisation
germination
life cycle
pollination
seed dispersal

Think back

Think back to the life cycle of a plant that you studied on page 18. How many stages did it have? Name the stages.

We have learned that flowering plants need to be pollinated to produce seeds, making the life cycle complete.

The pollen needs to reach the ovary of the female part of the flower. The pollen lands on the sticky stigma and the pollen nucleus travels down the style until it reaches the ovary. When the pollen nucleus joins with the ovule this is called fertilisation.

Once the ovule has been fertilised, a seed is produced.

A seed needs to find a place to grow that provides all the things it needs. The seed needs warmth and water, and then it starts the next part of its journey through the life cycle.

When the seed starts to grow, we say the seed has germinated. You will learn about this process in the next lesson.

Look at the diagram of the life cycle opposite. Remember that a life cycle shows a circle of events.

At what point in the life cycle is the flowering plant pollinated?

Talk about the different ways that seeds can be dispersed.

■ For more activities, go to Workbook 5 page 34.

Think about the processes we have learned about:

- pollination
- fertilisation
- seed production
- seed dispersal
- germination.

Study the diagram of the life cycle of flowering plants.

Identify the processes taking place at A, B, C, D and E.

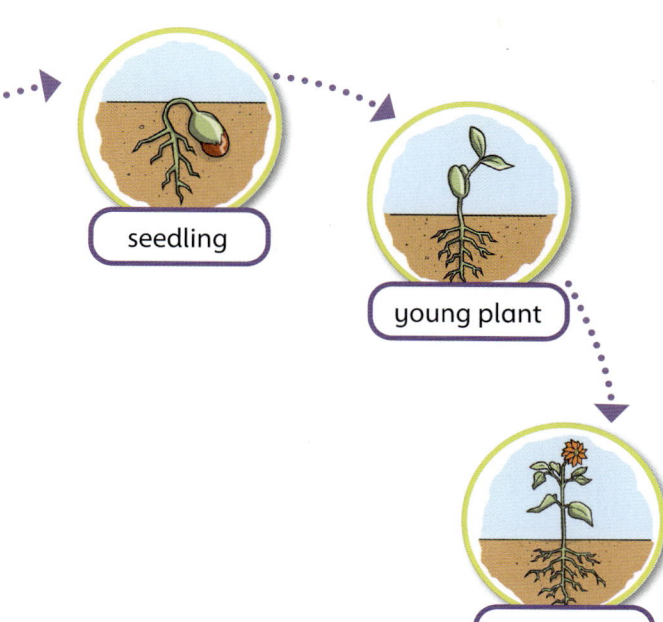

E

seeds

seedling

young plant

D

fruit or seed pods

adult plant

C

B

A

Science fact

Some plants die off each year. These plants are called annuals. Other plants live and keep making seeds every year. These plants are called perennials.

Displaying the life cycle of a flowering plant

1. Produce a poster-sized version of the life cycle. Add pictures from the internet of each of the stages.
2. Label the processes.
3. Add notes to explain why each process is important to flowering plants.

Stretch zone

Research and write a short report on the advantages and disadvantages of self-fertilisation for flowering plants.

Key idea

The life cycle of flowering plants passes through lots of stages, from seed production to adult plant with flowers.

1 Life Cycle and Growth of Flowering Plants

■ For more activities, go to Workbook 5 page 35.

Does seed germination need light?

In this lesson you will investigate whether seeds need light for germination.

Key words

germination

variable

Think back

What happens to a seed when it germinates?

Draw a picture of a seed that has just germinated.

After seeds have been dispersed, they begin the next stage of the life cycle, which is germination. This is where the seed develops and grows under the ground and then breaks through the surface into the air to become a seedling.

Sunny garden   Concrete path   Oasis

Study the photographs.

Which show plants growing? Discuss why plants are not growing in the other areas.

Plants need something to grow in. This is called a growth medium and helps the plants to stay upright and provides the nutrients and water they need. The most common growth medium is soil. Soil must be looked after.

Soil can be damaged by removing the plants that stop it washing away or by planting too many plants so all of the nutrients are used up. Sometimes pollution can wash into soil.

Nutrients and water can be added and farmers can build terraces to stop the soil being washed away.

■ For more activities, go to Workbook 5 page 36.

Investigating if seeds need light to germinate

You are going to plant some seeds and test whether they need light to help them to germinate.

Any small pot or even eggshells can be used

1 Fill six small pots with compost. Add some identical seeds to each pot.

2 Label three pots 'light'. Label the other three pots 'dark'.

3 Add the same amount of water to each pot so the compost is damp.

4 Place the 'dark' pots in a dark, warm place. Place the 'light' pots in a light, warm place.

5 Check the pots every day. Keep the compost moist.

6 Design a table and record your observations.

7 What is your conclusion? Did the seeds need light to help them to germinate?

Decide which were the control variables in your seed investigation.

What was the independent variable?

You should have found that the seeds did not need light to germinate. Seeds need to be able to germinate in the dark. They germinate under the soil and no light can reach them.

Science fact

Different seeds take different times to germinate. Asparagus can take up to 21 days. Cress seeds can germinate in just a couple of days or even as soon as 24 hours.

Stretch zone

Research some seeds from different fruits.
Which ones germinate the quickest? Record the information in a table.

Key idea

Seeds do not need light to germinate.

■ For more activities, go to Workbook 5 page 37.

Does seed germination need water and warmth?

In this lesson you will explore if seeds need water and warmth to germinate.

Key words
control
germination
variable
warmth

Think back

Do plants need light to help them to germinate?

Scientists believe that seeds need water and warmth to help them to germinate.

You are going to test both of these ideas. In your investigation you will be using the same type of seeds, the same number of seeds and the same amount of soil.

Discuss the control variables for your investigation. Why are they important?

How important are water and warmth for seed germination?

Below is a list of all the variable combinations you will need to test:

- pot 1: both water and warmth
- pot 2: water but no warmth
- pot 3: no water but warmth
- pot 4: no water and no warmth.

Note: To make sure that the seeds do not have warmth, we can put them in a fridge.

1   Place the same amount of soil in each of your four pots and plant ten grass seeds in each.

2   Label and date each pot.

3   Place each pot in one of the four different conditions. Do not overwater the seeds that require water. (Sprinkle with water every three or four days so they do not dry out.)

4   Observe the pots every day.

38

■ For more activities, go to Workbook 5 page 38.

5 Copy and complete the table below by writing 'grown' or 'not grown'. When the grass appears above the surface of the soil, you can write 'grown'.

	Grown/Not grown			
	Pot 1	Pot 2	Pot 3	Pot 4
Week 1				
Week 2				

6 What are your conclusions?

Did the seeds need water, warmth or both to germinate?

7 Design and make an information leaflet for gardeners about seed germination like the one below.

Include a description of your investigation.

Share your conclusions and advice about germinating seeds.

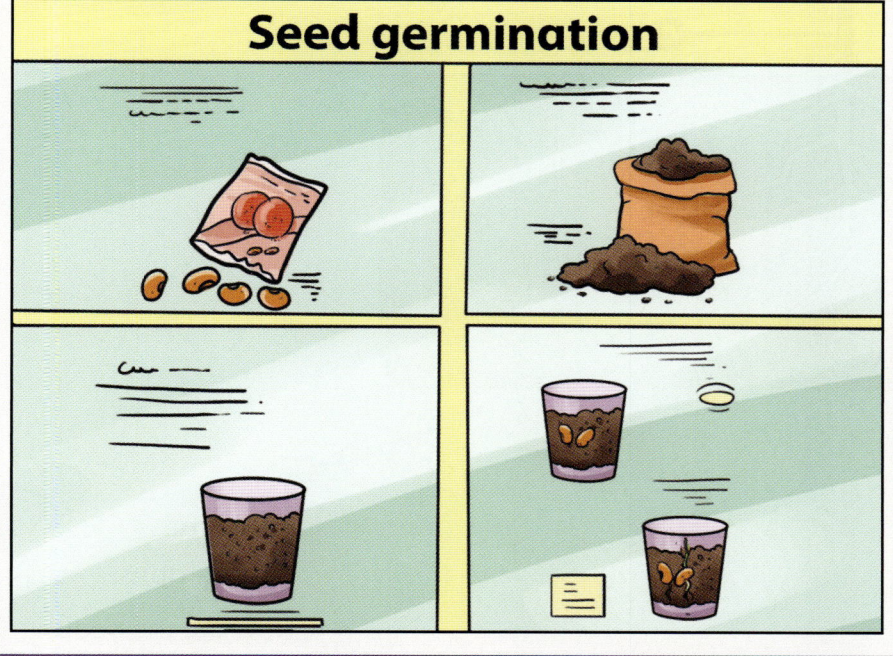

Seed germination

■ For more activities, go to Workbook 5 page 39.

Science fact

Water enters seeds through a tiny hole called the micropyle. You can see this hole with a hand lens.

Stretch zone

Some gardeners scratch the surface of seeds or soak them overnight before they are planted. They believe that this helps water to enter the seed.

Plan an investigation to test one of these ideas.

Key idea

Seeds need water and warmth to germinate.

Plants and water

In this lesson you will understand that plants need water to grow.

Think back

Discuss the diagram of the plant.

Name the parts labelled A, B, C and D.

Study the photographs

How are the healthy and unhealthy plants different?

Talk about some of the reasons why the plant on the right is not healthy.

■ For more activities, go to Workbook 5 page 40.

Investigating if plants need water

A student has left a plant on a windowsill, and is wondering why it stopped looking healthy. The teacher told the student that they must have forgotten to give the plant water.

You are going to check to see if the teacher was right.

1 Plan an investigation to find out if plants do need water.

   You can plant seeds and then grow the plants or use the seedlings you grew earlier in the unit.

   Once you have identical seedlings in at least two pots you can:

   • decide on what you are going to change – your independent variable

   • decide what you are going to measure or observe – your dependent variable.

   Now make a list of all of the things you will keep the same – your control variables.

2 Design a table so you can record your results.

3 Grow your seedlings and observe them every day.

   If you are going to measure them, make sure you do this accurately and the same way every time.

4 Study the pattern of your results. What does it tell you about plants and water?

5 Design a large poster about your investigation and findings. Display it in the classroom.

6 Walk around to learn from other peoples' displays.

Plants need water to grow and stay healthy. Water keeps their leaves and stems upright. The nutrients they need for growth enter the plant in water and move around the plant in water.

A plant without water will droop. This is called wilting.

Stretch zone

Research how plants are adapted to live in very wet areas. Draw an example to share with the class.

■ For more activities, go to Workbook 5 page 41.

Science fact

Some plants are adapted to live in very dry habitats. They may store water and have long and wide roots to search for water. Many have needles rather than leaves.

Key idea

Plants need water to grow. If they don't have water they will wilt.

Plants and light

In this lesson you will understand that plants need energy from light to grow.

Key words

energy

light

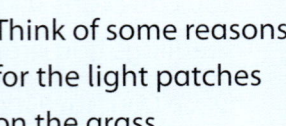

Look at the picture.

Think of some reasons for the light patches on the grass.

Use clues you can see in the picture to decide the most likely explanation.

The farmers who own the land think that tents may have blocked the light and the grass hasn't grown as well. If plants needed light, this would make sense.

 Do plants need light to grow?

You will plan an investigation to find out if the farmers have the correct idea about the patches on the grass.

1 You will have some identical plants in two different pots. Label one pot 'light' and the other pot 'no light'.

2 What will be your independent, dependent and control variables?

3 Decide how you will keep the plants in the 'dark' pot out of the light. Place the 'light' pot in a sunny place.

4 Observe the plants in each pot every day for a week. Are you going to measure them? Can you take photographs?

5 Design a results table so you can record your results.

6 What do your results tell you about plants and light?

7 Write a conclusion about why there were patches of yellow grass after the camping festival.

In this investigation, we discovered that plants left in darkness die fairly quickly. Our conclusion as scientists is that light is essential for the growth of plants.

■ For more activities, go to Workbook 5 page 42.

Why is light so important to plants?

Plants use the energy from light to help them to make food. This takes place in the leaves.

A person noticed that their plant seemed to grow towards the light.

You can investigate to see if this is true.

Do plants grow towards the light?

1. Make your own plant maze using a cardboard box and card.
2. Place some seedlings in a pot at the bottom of the box.
3. Cut a hole at the opposite end of the maze. Close the box so the only light comes through the hole.
4. Leave the plant maze in the light and check it every day. Keep the seedlings watered. Observe what happens.
5. Did the plant grow towards the light?

Science fact

Plant shoots grow towards the light and plant roots grow downwards due to gravity.

Key idea

Light is essential for the growth of green plants.

■ For more activities, go to Workbook 5 page 43.

Can plants have too much light?

In this lesson you will investigate whether plants can have too much light.

Key words

growth

light

variable

Think back

What do plants need to help them to grow. Make a list.

Do you think more sunlight will help a plant to grow better? Can a plant have too much sunlight? Share your ideas.

You should have sunlight on your list. Plants use energy from the Sun to help them to make their food. When they do this they make a gas called oxygen as a waste material. This is sent out through holes in the leaves.

Look at what the boy in the picture is asking. You can plan an investigation to help him find out.

Scientists can use their knowledge that plants make oxygen. The better the plants use the Sun's energy, the more oxygen they will make. Oxygen is a gas. It can be seen as bubbles if the plant is underwater.

Will this plant grow better if it has more sunlight?

Science fact

Only 1–2% of the energy reaching Earth from the Sun is used by plants. This still traps enough energy for almost every food chain on the planet.

Talk about the investigation on the next page. Which variables would you keep the same? What are you altering? What are you measuring?

■ For more activities, go to Workbook 5 page 44.

Does increasing the light help plants to make food?

You will use pond weed to investigate whether increasing the light helps plants make even more food (energy). Pond weed grows in water and uses light energy to make food and oxygen.

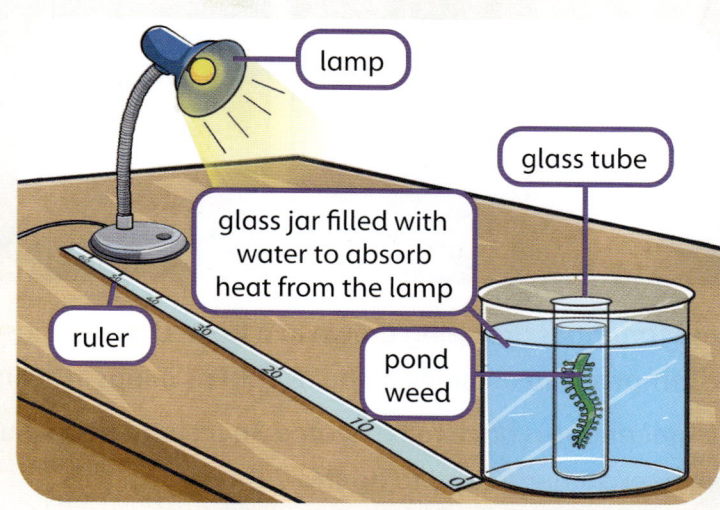

lamp

glass tube

glass jar filled with water to absorb heat from the lamp

ruler

pond weed

1   Half fill a glass tube with water. Place your pond weed into the tube, with the cut end upwards. Gently push the pond weed down.

2   Top up the tube with water and stand it in a jar of water.

3   Place a lamp 10 cm from the pond weed. Switch the lamp on. You should see bubbles around the pond weed after 1–2 minutes.

4   Count the number of bubbles that escape from the pond weed in one minute and record this in a table.

5   Move the lamp to 20 cm from the pond weed. Wait five minutes to allow the pond weed to get used to its surroundings. Count the number of bubbles for one minute and record this in your table.

6   Repeat the experiment – moving the lamp 10 cm further away from the pond weed each time until the lamp is one metre away from the pond weed.

7   Write up your investigation as a scientific report.

Include a diagram, your prediction, a results table and your conclusions.

8   Look up your conclusions on the internet to check if other scientists have found the same.

Predict what will happen if you move the lamp further away from the pond weed.

 Be a scientist

Scientists regularly look up information in secondary sources to check that their results and conclusions are sensible.

▶ page 8

Key idea

Plants need just the right amount of light.

■ For more activities, go to Workbook 5 page 45.

Plants and warmth

In this lesson you will investigate if plants need warmth to grow.

Key words
growth
warmth

These tomatoes are being grown in a heated greenhouse in Iceland. The temperature outside can be as cold as minus 10°C in winter.

The greenhouses have to be heated. In Iceland people use hot water from deep underground to do this.

What would happen to the tomato plants if they were grown outside in Iceland?

Do plants grow better in the warmth or the cold?

You can investigate whether plants grow better in the warmth.

1 Take two identical plants. Record the height, number of leaves and number of flowers of both plants. Write these into a results table.

2 Place one plant in a light but cool place. Place the other in a light and warm place.

3 Water both plants and keep them well watered. Place a thermometer next to each plant.

4 Observe and measure the plants every day for a week. Record what you see. Record the temperatures.

5 What differences did you see? What is your conclusion?

Science fact

Some plants are adapted to live in very cold habitats. Taller plants drop their leaves when it is coldest and others have thick waxy coverings to protect their leaves. Many plants are small to lower water loss in cold, windy weather.

■ For more activities, go to Workbook 5 page 46.

In previous lessons you found out that plants need light and water for healthy growth. They also need warmth. Plants grow faster in warm conditions than in cold conditions.

This can be seen in the graph below.

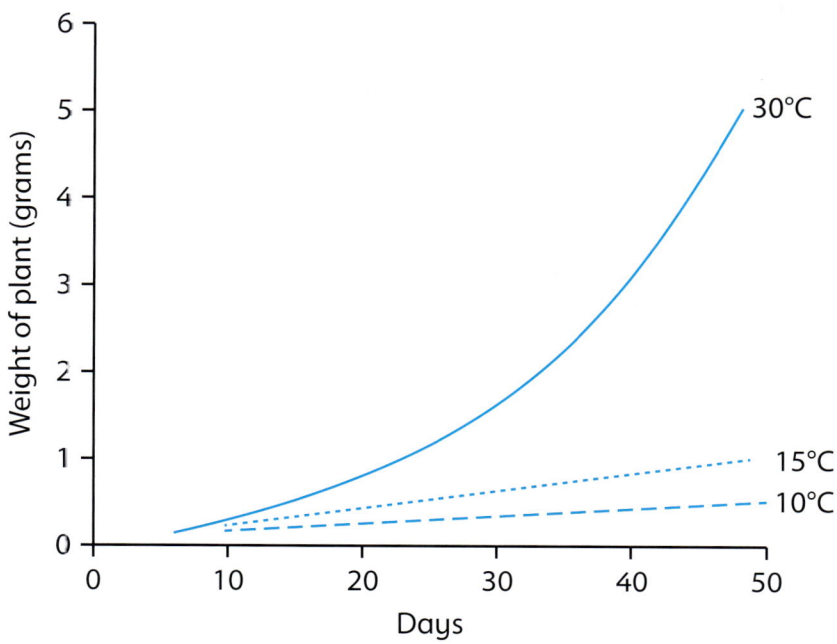

Look at the graph. How was plant growth measured in the collection of this information?

Which temperature showed the most plant growth?

Predict how much the plants would grow after 40 days at 25°C.

Science fact

Each plant has its own ideal growth temperature. If a plant gets too hot, it can stop growing or even die.

Stretch zone

Plants adapted to live in hot habitats have to lower the amount of water they lose or find ways to get water. Research three ways they do this. Present your ideas to the class.

Check how much you know.
Try the questions on pages 48–49.

Key idea

Plants need the right temperature as well as the right amount of water and light.

■ For more activities, go to Workbook 5 page 47.

What have I learned about the life cycle and growth of flowering plants?

1 Which of these is NOT a way that seeds are dispersed? Circle your answer.

animals   gravity   water   wind

2 Decide whether the following statements are true or false. Circle your choice.

Insects are the only things that can pollinate a flowering plant.   true   false

Flowers do not attract insects.   true   false

Pollen can be transported to other plants in many ways.   true   false

3 Look at the life cycle of a flowering plant. Write the name of each process in the correct box. Use the words in the word box.

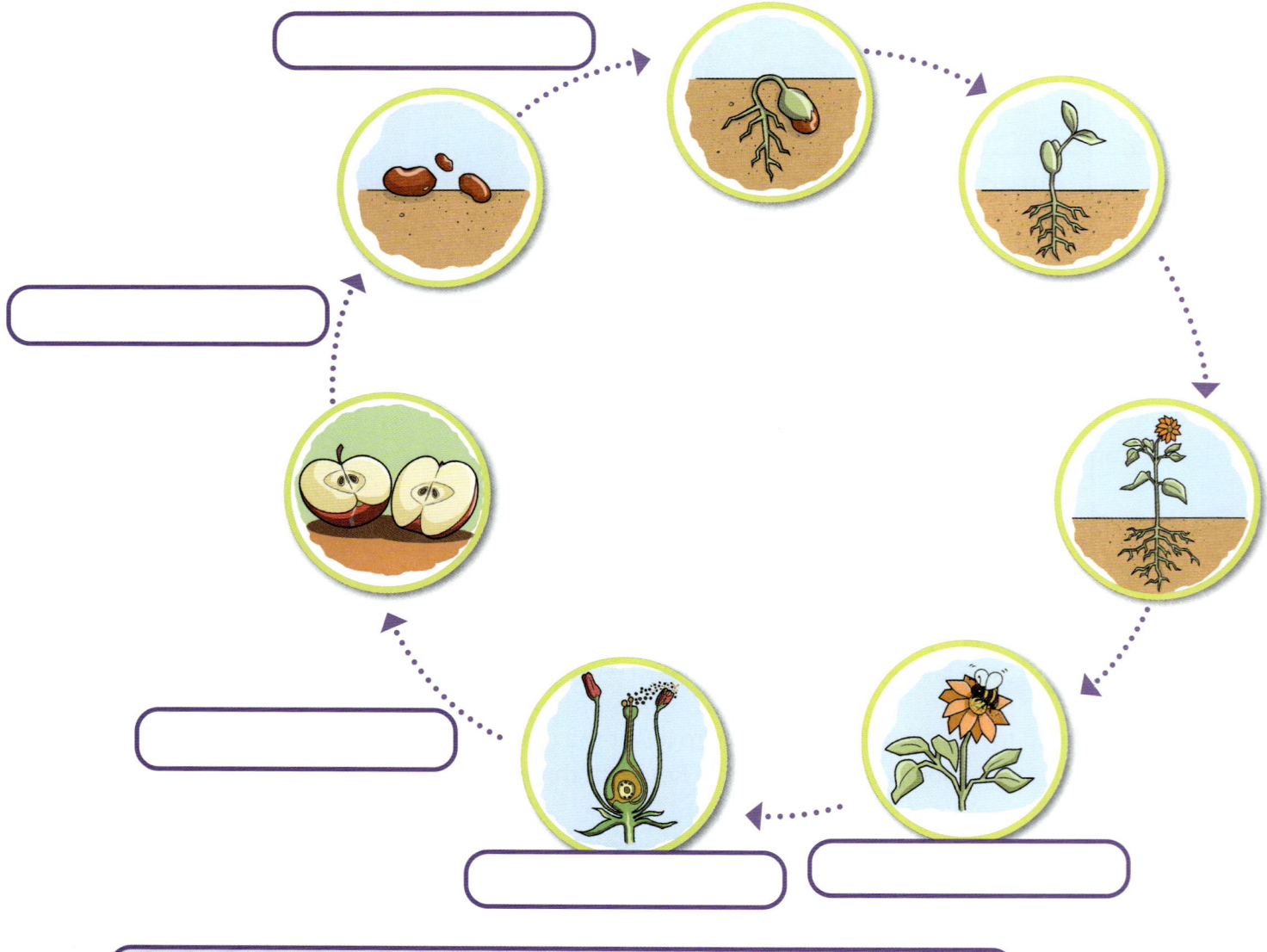

fertilisation   germination   pollination   seed dispersal   seed production

■ For more activities, go to Workbook 5 page 48.

4 Look at the flowers shown below.

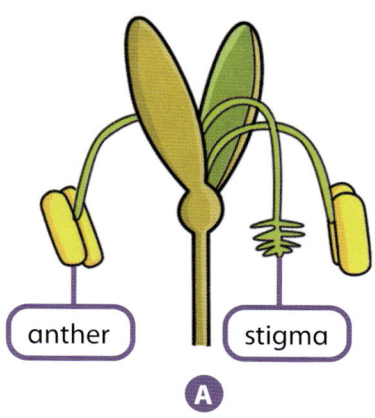

A

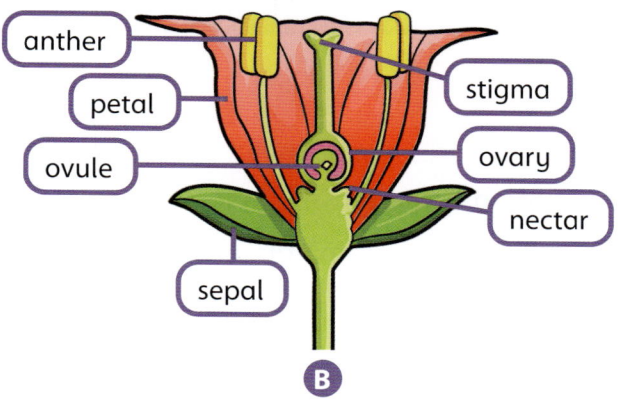

B

a Which flower is adapted to encourage wind pollination? _____

b Explain two ways in which it is adapted for this type of pollination.

_____

_____

5 A student investigated the effect of light on plants.

a Which gas is made when green plants are in light? _____

b Look at the table.

Distance between light source and plant (cm)	Amount of gas produced (bubbles per minute)
10	25
40	18
60	12
100	8

What do the results tell you about light and plants?

_____

_____

c Is the distance between the light source and the plant the independent or dependent variable in the investigation? Circle your choice in the question.

d Is the amount of gas produced the independent or dependent variable in the investigation? Circle your choice in the question.

■ For more activities, go to Workbook 5 page 49.

Life Cycles and Growth of Animals and Humans

In this unit you will:

- revise the life processes – movement, growth, reproduction, breathing, feeding, using senses
- explore the life cycles of mammals, amphibians, insects and birds
- describe the changes as humans grow and develop to old age.

adolescent   amphibian   baby   bird   chrysalis   feeding   growth   insect   larva   life cycle   living   mammal   movement   reproduction   tadpole

How are these two animals linked?

Discuss any parts of the life cycle of these animals you know about.

chimpanzee

rat

gorilla

mouse

Discuss the animals in the photographs.

How are they the same?

How are they different?

What do they all have to do to stay alive?

Science fact

There are at least 6 000 000 kinds of animal in the world making up the animal kingdom!

These dolphins are alive and healthy.

Discuss with a partner what dolphins have to do to stay healthy.

51

■ For more activities, go to Workbook 5 pages 50–51.

Life processes

In this lesson you will revise the life processes.

Think back

List two life processes you have used today. What would happen if animals were not able to carry out the life processes?

To stay alive, living things must be able to carry out life processes.
In animals, these include the following.

Key words
breathing
feeding
growth
movement
reproduction
senses

Which life processes can you see happening in the photograph? What will happen if the lioness catches the antelope? Why is this important to the lioness?

Movement
Allows animals to move to find or catch food. Animals can move to avoid danger such as predators, floods or fires.

Growth
Important so that animals can be born small and then develop to be stronger and larger.

Reproduction
Allows animals to make copies of themselves (offspring) because an individual animal cannot live forever.

Breathing
Gets oxygen into the animal so it can be used to break down food. Breathing also allows carbon dioxide to be removed from the body.

Feeding
This is how animals take in nutrients, which are broken down (digested) to give raw materials and energy.

Using senses
Animals use their senses to detect what is around them, to help them to find food and stay safe.

■ For more activities, go to Workbook 5 page 52.

Observing animal movement

You will carry out a survey of animal movement in your local area.

1. Observe an animal in your area for 15 to 30 minutes.

2. Use a key or identification book to name the animal.

3. Design and complete a table to record how the animal moves. Use words such as fly, crawl, hop, walk, jump, burrow, run or slither.

4. Present your findings to the class. Use a poster or presentation.

5. Compare your results with others in the class. What was the most common type of movement?

Be a scientist

Scientists often set time limits on observations and surveys. They also compare what happens in day time with night-time.

▶ page 10

Discuss what would happen to the animals if they were not able to move.

Science fact

A cheetah can run at speeds of up to 76 kilometres per hour. That is fast compared to a person, but slow compared to a peregrine falcon. When it is diving for prey, this bird can reach speeds of up to 200 kilometres per hour!

Key idea

Animals need to carry out life processes to allow them to stay alive and make new versions of themselves.

Stretch zone

Design and carry out a survey of your area to find examples of animals using another life process, such as feeding or using their senses. Write a short report to share your ideas.

■ For more activities, go to Workbook 5 page 53.

Living or non-living?

In this lesson you will explore the differences between living and non-living things.

Key words

living/non-living

mammal

Think back

Make a list of all the life processes you know.

Animals are living things because they breathe, eat and drink, move, grow and reproduce. They also use their senses.

Plants are also living things. They require food and water to grow. They do not need to move to get food because they make food using energy from the Sun. However, they do move by turning towards light.

Plants also reproduce to make new plants.

When plants and animals die, they are no longer living but they once lived.

Look at the photographs. Discuss which things you think are living and which are non-living.

Which photograph shows something that was once living, but is no longer living?

Survey of living and non-living things

You are going to plan a survey of your local area.

1   Find ten examples of living things and ten examples of non-living things. Also record five things that were once living.

2   Take photographs or draw your examples.

3   Present your findings as a large poster. One half should be labelled 'living' and the other half 'non-living'.

Place examples of once-living things at the bottom of the 'living' part of your poster.

4   Your teacher will help you to make a class display or exhibition of all of the posters.

Science fact

Some rocks are made from once-living creatures. Limestone can have fossils of shellfish in them. We still call rocks non-living though.

54

■ For more activities, go to Workbook 5 page 54.

Movement is an important life process. All living things move.
Some non-living things move but cannot do this on their own.

 Do plants move?

You will investigate movement in plants.

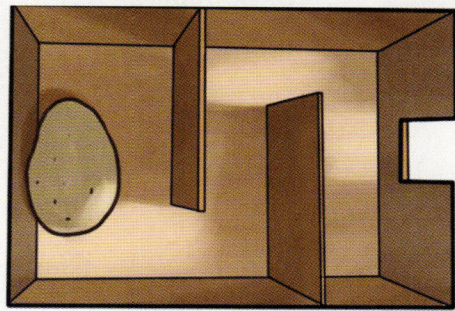

1   Set up a potato maze as shown in the picture.

2   Place your potato at the far end of the maze.

3   Put a lid on the box and place it in a sunny place.

4   Write a prediction of what you will see over the next few days.

5   Observe your maze every two days for about two weeks. Take the lid off to see what is happening but place it back quickly. Measure how long your potato plant is.

6   Draw what happens to the potato. Label your drawing.

7   Write your conclusions.

Was your prediction correct?

Do plants move?

Discuss how each of these animals moves.

Describe each one to your partner. Use words such as creep, crawl, slither and jump.

Key idea

Living things carry out all life processes. Non-living things do not.

 Stretch zone

Many mammals live on land. Research one mammal that lives in the sea and one that flies. Describe how these animals move.

■ For more activities, go to Workbook 5 page 55.

Comparing plants and animals

In this lesson you will discover that plants and animals have some of the same life processes and can adapt to their environment.

Key words
adapted
life process

Think back

Think about the differences between living and non-living things.

Look at the picture of the plants. Which plant shows some damage? What do you think damaged the plant? What problems does the plant have now?

Look at the picture. Would you ever see this happening?

Plants have similar living processes to animals but there are differences.

How plants are similar to animals	How plants are different from animals
Plants need food and water.	Plants do not move from place to place but can move towards sunlight.
Plants grow and reproduce. Flowering plants do this by producing seeds, which grow into new plants.	Plants make their own food from water, air and sunlight.

Why is the making of seeds called sexual reproduction? What other type of reproduction do some plants carry out?

■ For more activities, go to Workbook 5 page 56.

Animals and plants can adapt to live in their habitats. The adaptations allow them to carry out their life processes. Habitats might be dry or wet, hot or cold, shaded or sunny or a mixture of all of these.

Hot and dry habitat

Compare how plants and animals adapt to dry habitats

1 Research some plants and animals that live in hot, dry habitats such as deserts.

2 Make a list of the problems these living things face.

3 Choose one plant and one animal to study in detail.

4 Collect information about how they are adapted to carry out their life processes.

5 Do the plant and animal have any adaptations that are similar?

6 Produce a computer presentation to share your ideas with the class. Include pictures.

Finding out about scientists

Your teacher will invite in a scientist who studies plants or animals.

1 Work with your group to design three questions to ask the scientist. Try to find out about what the scientist studies and the techniques they use.

2 Listen carefully to the scientist and then ask your questions. Note down their answers.

3 Design a computer presentation to show people about the work of the scientist.

Stretch zone

Research the work of a famous scientist, such as Sir David Attenborough or a famous scientist from your country. Make a poster about the person and display it in your classroom.

Key idea

Plants need food and water and they grow and reproduce, but they are different from animals in some life processes.

■ For more activities, go to Workbook 5 page 57.

Reproduction in animals and humans

In this lesson you will explore how reproduction is an important life process.

Key words

characteristics
extinct
offspring
reproduce
species
vertebrate

Think back

Vertebrates are split into five smaller classes. Make a list of these classes and write down one animal from each class.

Animals and humans grow up and reproduce. They have offspring so that their species does not die out.

Humans produce only a few offspring. Some animals, like horses and cows, are the same. They care for their offspring while they are growing up.

Other animals, like fish and insects, produce lots of offspring. These animals leave their offspring to grow up on their own.

With a partner talk about how many adults and how many children there are in your families.

Can you think what would happen to your family if eventually no more children were born?

Thousands of fish eggs!

Different vertebrates produce different numbers of eggs.

Vertebrate class	Name of animal	Number of eggs
birds	robin	4–6
reptiles	crocodile	20–100
amphibians	frog	500–1000
fish	herring	20 000–40 000

Science fact

Twelve rabbits were introduced into Australia in 1859. Before that there were no rabbits there. In less than 100 years there were over 6 000 000! This huge increase in numbers caused a lot of damage to crops and habitats.

Which animal lays the fewest eggs?

Which animal lays the most eggs?

Discuss how the robin looks after its eggs. How is this different from the frog and the herring?

■ For more activities, go to Workbook 5 page 58.

Why animals reproduce

Individual animals cannot live forever. Before they die they must make new animals. This allows animals of the same type to survive. Animals of the same type are called a species.

As in plants, sexual reproduction allows characteristics from both parents to be passed on to their offspring. There is also a mixing of parent characteristics. This can lead to useful new characteristics.

If a species of animal is dying faster than young animals are being born, then this species will become extinct. It will never be seen on Earth again.

Species can become extinct naturally but also humans can speed up the process. They do this by hunting, polluting or destroying habitats.

Be a scientist

Scientists use resources such as the internet and books to carry out research, as well as doing their own investigations. These resources are called secondary sources of information.

▶ page 8

Researching extinct animals

Find out about one of these animals.
Use books, magazines or the internet.

1   Find out when it became extinct and why.

2   Produce a poster, including a timeline, explaining how the animal became extinct.

Western black rhinoceros

Steller's sea cow

Passenger pigeon

Pyrenean ibex

Tasmanian tiger

Dodo

Science fact

The Arabian oryx, which lived in the Middle East, became extinct in the wild in 1972. Some still lived in zoos. In 1982, thanks to the efforts of many people, it was re-introduced to the wild. Now there are over 1000 Arabian oryx.

Key idea

Animals reproduce to make new animals of the same species. If they did not, that species would become extinct.

Stretch zone

Produce an information leaflet explaining why reproduction is important and why humans need to protect animals so they do not become extinct.

■ For more activities, go to Workbook 5 page 59.

Life cycle of insects

In this lesson you will explore the life cycle of an insect.

Think back

Like plants, animals go through a series of changes as they grow and develop. This is called a life cycle.

Animals need to eat and drink to stay alive. They also move and grow. Animals do not live forever. They have to make new versions of themselves or that type of animal will die out. This is called reproduction. When animals reproduce, they make offspring.

Key words

chrysalis
egg
insect
larva
life cycle
offspring
pupa

Look at the photographs. How are these animals the same? How are they different?

Insects reproduce by laying eggs. The eggs hatch and the insect grows and changes until it becomes an adult. These changes are called a life cycle.

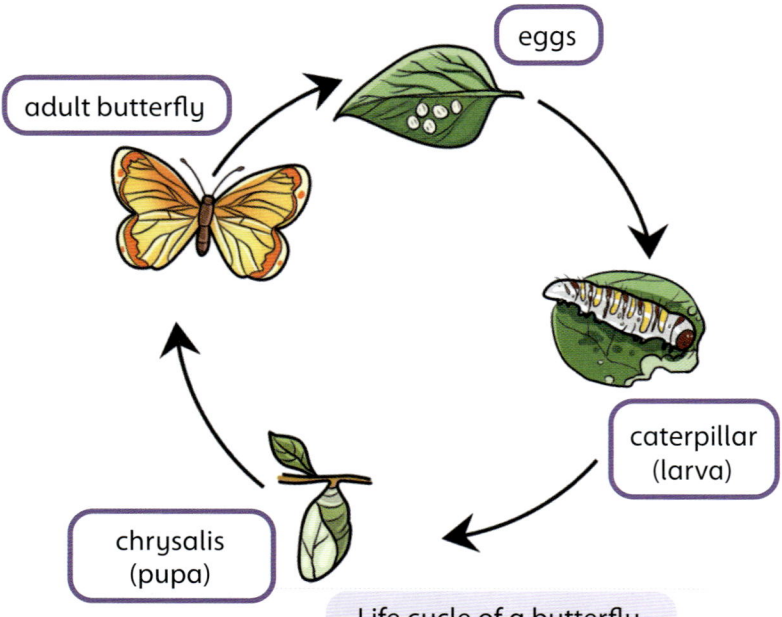

eggs

adult butterfly

caterpillar (larva)

chrysalis (pupa)

Life cycle of a butterfly

■ For more activities, go to Workbook 5 page 60.

The larva, called a caterpillar, eats and grows. The caterpillar eats by chewing leaves. It moves by crawling. When it has grown, the caterpillar forms a pupa or chrysalis. Inside the pupa the caterpillar changes into an adult butterfly.

Adult butterflies eat by sucking nectar through a long tube. They move by flying.

Studying the butterfly life cycle

1 Collect five caterpillars from leaves near your school.

Warning!

Check with your teacher before touching any plants or insects. Discuss why this is important.

2 Place the caterpillars into a tall glass container with a lid that has air holes. Add some of the leaves of the plant where you found the caterpillars. Keep them away from direct sunlight.

Be a scientist

Scientists often study animals in the laboratory rather than outside. This makes it easier to observe any changes and to record findings.

▶ page 10

3 Observe the caterpillars over the next few weeks. Draw any changes you see. Label the stages of the life cycle, using the diagram opposite to help you.

4 Time how long it takes for the caterpillar to forms its chrysalis. Then time how long it takes to develop into a butterfly. Compare the times with other groups and calculate a mean average for each stage.

5 Write the times for the two stages onto your drawing.

6 Once butterflies appear, let them fly away.

Why is it important to provide the caterpillars with leaves? Why must you let the butterflies fly away after your investigation?

Stretch zone

Research the life cycle of a dragonfly. Draw a diagram to show how it is different from the life cycle of a butterfly.

Key ideas

- Insects have to eat, drink, move, grow and reproduce.
- Insects have a life cycle that starts with eggs.

2 Life Cycles and Growth of Animals and Humans

61

Life cycle of amphibians and birds

In this lesson you will explore the life cycle of an amphibian and a bird.

Think back

How did the life cycle of the butterfly start?

Key words

amphibian
bird
egg
froglet
gills
tadpole

Life cycle of a frog

Amphibians such as frogs have a life cycle that involves a water stage and a land stage. Adult frogs lay soft eggs in water.

Talk about the photograph. What does it show? Have you ever seen these in nature?

adult frog

eggs

froglet

tadpole with legs

tadpole

Life cycle of a frog

A tadpole hatches from the egg and eats and grows. The tadpole eats by chewing plants. It moves by swimming and it breathes through gills. When it grows, the tadpole loses its tail and grows legs. It changes to a froglet and then an adult frog.

Adult frogs eat by catching insects. They move by hopping and they breathe through their skin and lungs.

Science fact

Frogs do not need to drink water. They can absorb it through their skin.

62

■ For more activities, go to Workbook 5 page 62.

Life cycle of a chicken

Birds also lay eggs. The eggs have a waterproof shell as they are laid on land. This stops them from drying out. When the young birds hatch, they are known as chicks.

Chicks eat what their parents eat. Birds in a nest often need to be fed until they can fly to find their own food.

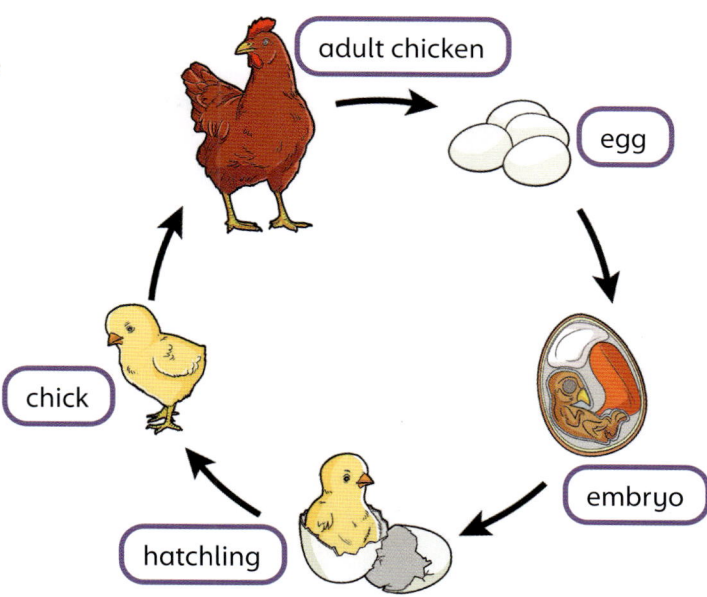

Life cycle of a chicken

Comparing animal life cycles

How are the life cycles of insects, amphibians and birds the same? How are they different?

1   Use a table like the one below to list the similarities and differences for each life cycle.

Life cycle	How is this the same as the other life cycles?	How is this different from the other life cycles?
insect – butterfly		
insect – dragonfly		
amphibian – frog		
bird – chicken		

2   Compare your table with another group. Were their ideas different?

3   Make an information leaflet to share your ideas.

Key ideas

- Amphibians and birds have to eat, drink, move, grow and reproduce.
- Amphibians and birds have a life cycle that starts with eggs.

■ For more activities, go to Workbook 5 page 63.

Life cycle of mammals

In this lesson you will explore the life cycle of mammals.

Key words

adolescent

adult

baby

child

colt

foal

Look at the parent and their offspring. How are they the same? How are they different? What is the offspring doing?

Mammals are covered by hair or fur. They have offspring that are born alive. The offspring are fed at first on milk made by the mother.

The young horse grows from an egg inside the mother for 11 months. The time the offspring takes to grow before it is born is called the gestation period. After it is born it is fed milk. As it grows it becomes bigger and stronger and can eat what the mother eats.

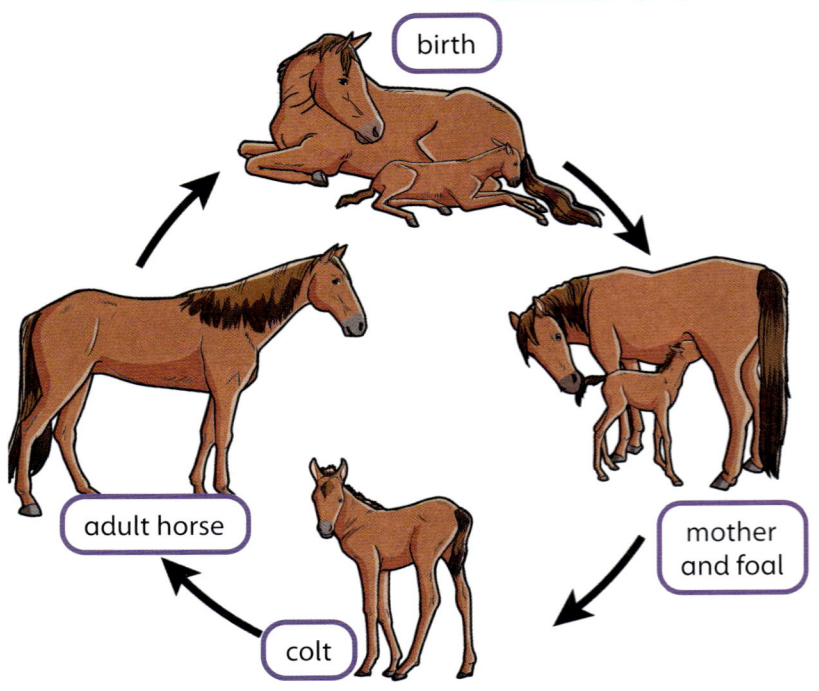

birth

mother and foal

colt

adult horse

Life cycle of a mammal

Stretch zone

Research the life cycle of a sheep and a panda. Draw the cycles and include their gestation periods and the names given to the young animals.

■ For more activities, go to Workbook 5 page 64.

Making a mammal life cycle disc

You are going to make a model of a life cycle using two paper plates.

1 Divide one paper plate into four sections.

2 Cut a wedge-shaped section out of the other plate.

3 Choose a mammal and use the plates to show its life cycle:

- Draw four stages of the life cycle onto the bottom, divided plate.
- Fix the top plate onto the bottom plate using a paper fastener.
- Label the life cycle by drawing a title and picture on the top plate.

4 Now share your plate with other people. Ask others to predict each step of the life cycle before you turn the top plate.

Humans have a life cycle too

As humans get older, we change and go through different stages.

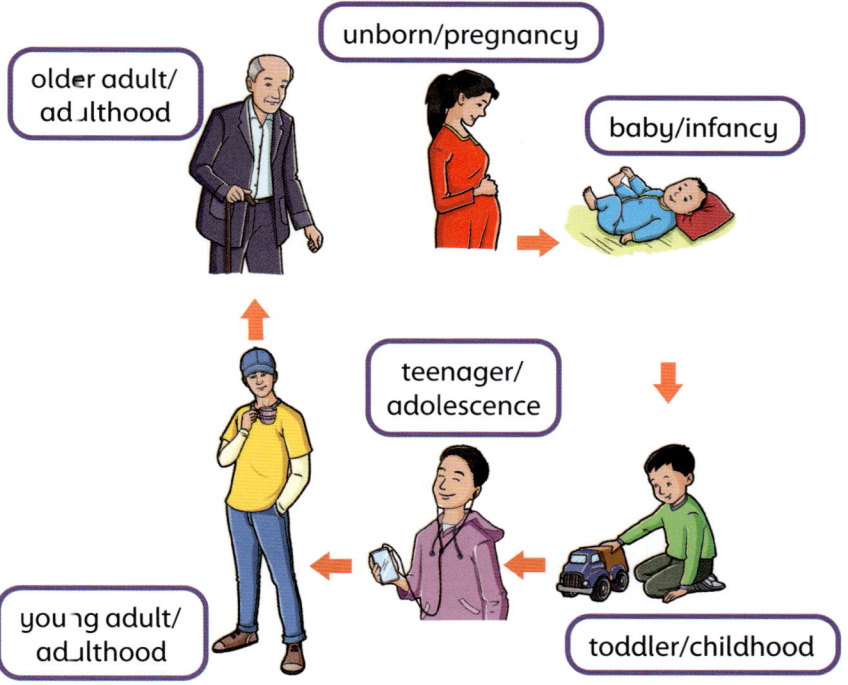

Life cycle of a human

Talk about people you know who are at different stages in the human life cycle. Which stage are you at?

Key idea

Mammals have a life cycle where the offspring are born alive and are fed on milk when they are young.

The gestation period for humans is about nine months.

Adolescence is when young people start to grow and develop into adults. It is sometimes called the teenage stage.

■ For more activities, go to Workbook 5 page 65.

Human growth

In this lesson you will describe the changes as humans grow.

Key words

grow

reproduce

Think back

Humans have a gestation period of nine months. What is a gestation period?

Having enough food to eat allows our bodies to grow. This baby will grow up into an adult. Adults can have babies of their own because their bodies have developed and matured.

1 three months old

2

3

4

5

6

Look at the photographs of people at different stages of their lives. With a partner, estimate each person's age.

Write the ages on an age line, from 0 to 90 years old.

Be a scientist

Scientists estimate many things. This means they work out a possible answer based on information they already have.

▶ page 8

■ For more activities, go to Workbook 5 page 66.

Investigating how much babies grow

Doctors and nurses monitor babies by measuring them. This tells them how well the baby is developing. They compare the growth with an average, expected growth, as shown in this table.

Month	Girls (female)		Boys (male)	
	Weight (kg)	Length (cm)	Weight (kg)	Length (cm)
1	4.2	53.6	4.5	54.6
2	5.1	57.0	5.6	58.4
3	5.9	59.7	6.4	61.4
4	6.4	62.0	7.0	63.7
5	6.9	64.0	7.5	65.8
6	7.3	65.8	7.9	67.6
7	7.6	67.3	8.3	69.0
8	7.9	68.8	8.6	70.6
9	8.2	70.1	8.9	71.9

1 Look for patterns in the data shown in the table to help you to compare changes in length and weight as female and male babies develop.

2 Decide whether females or males tend to grow the most over the first six months.

3 Present your conclusions as a poster. Include a graph of either changes in length or changes in weight as evidence to support your ideas.

Be a scientist

Scientists describe facts, measurements and observations as data. They look for patterns in data to help them to make sense of investigations.

▶ page 7

All animals grow and reproduce. Humans grow up to become adults. Adults are able to reproduce and have families of their own.

Stretch zone

Research the stages of human growth. Write two or three key points about how humans develop at each stage.

Key idea

Humans grow and develop from babies to mature adults, and are then able to reproduce.

Check how much you know.
Try the questions on pages 68–69.

■ For more activities, go to Workbook 5 page 67.

What have I learned about the lives of animals and humans?

1 Circle the letter that shows the correct life cycle for a butterfly.

    A eggs, nymph, adult

    B eggs, chick, adult

    C eggs, larva, pupa, adult

2 Tick the words that are processes of life.

breathing ☐	falling ☐	feeding ☐
movement ☐	reproduction ☐	riding ☐

3 **a** Label the life cycle of the frog. Write the correct letter in the boxes.

    b Label the life cycle of the chicken. Write the correct letter in the boxes.

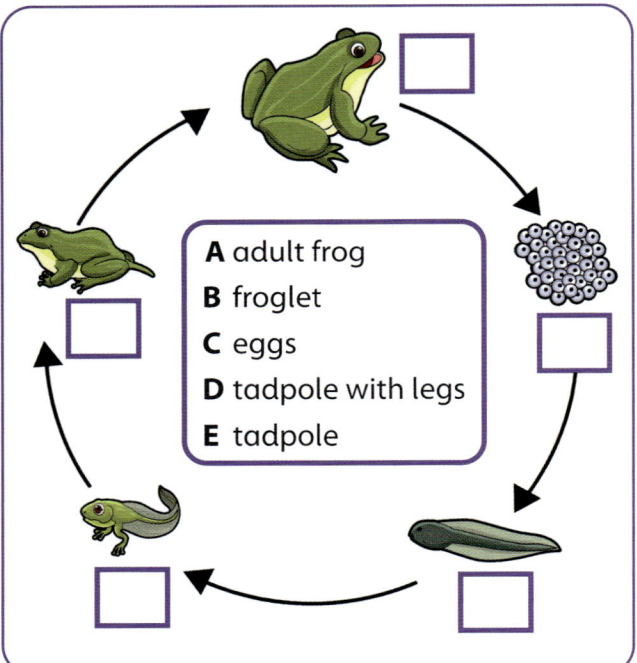

A adult frog
B froglet
C eggs
D tadpole with legs
E tadpole

A hatchling
B chick
C egg
D adult chicken
E embryo

4 Write in the missing phases in the life cycle of a butterfly.

egg ⟶ _____ ⟶ _____ ⟶ _____

■ For more activities, go to Workbook 5 page 68.

5 Underline the correct phase of the human life cycle.

    a This is the phase before a baby has been born:

        baby   adolescence   adult   pregnancy   older age

    b People at this phase often have grey hair and wrinkles:

        baby   adolescence   adult   pregnancy   older age

    c At this phase children are changing into adults:

        baby   adolescence   adult   pregnancy   older age

6 Study the table below.

Type of animal	How many observed in 30 minutes	How the animal moved
birds	26	flying
lizards	16	walking
snails	6	sliding
fish	19	swimming

    a Which type of animal was the most common during the observation time?

    _____

    b Which type of animal was the least common during the observation time?

    _____

    c What was the total number of animals observed in 30 minutes?

    _____

    d Write down one type of animal movement that was not observed during the investigation.

    _____

■ For more activities, go to Workbook 5 page 69.

3 Properties and Changes of Materials

In this unit you will:

- compare and group materials according to their properties
- investigate the reasons for particular uses of materials
- understand the difference between a reversible and an irreversible change
- explore how solids can be mixed and how it is often possible to separate them again
- know about changes that happen when some solids are added to water
- understand how some solids that do not dissolve or react with water can be separated by filtering
- explore the energy changes in some reactions.

dissolve   insoluble
irreversible   mixture
property   reaction
reversible   separate
soluble   solute
solution

Science fact

Fireworks were first made in China over 2000 years ago. They work when chemicals burn very quickly. Different chemicals give the fireworks the different colours.

Can this metal be made back into a solid?

Discuss why some things can go back to how they started and others cannot.

What will happen to the trees after the fire has gone out?

Can you imagine what the trees will look like?

Comparing and exploring the uses of materials

In this lesson you will compare materials and explore why they are used for particular things.

Key words
electrical conductivity
property
thermal conductivity

Think back

What is the property of a material? Find a hard, a soft, a smooth, a rough and a transparent object in the room.

The pictures shows different materials that you might have used in previous lessons. The property of a material describes how the material looks, feels and how it can be used.

Look at each of the materials in the pictures.

With a partner, describe at least one property of each material.

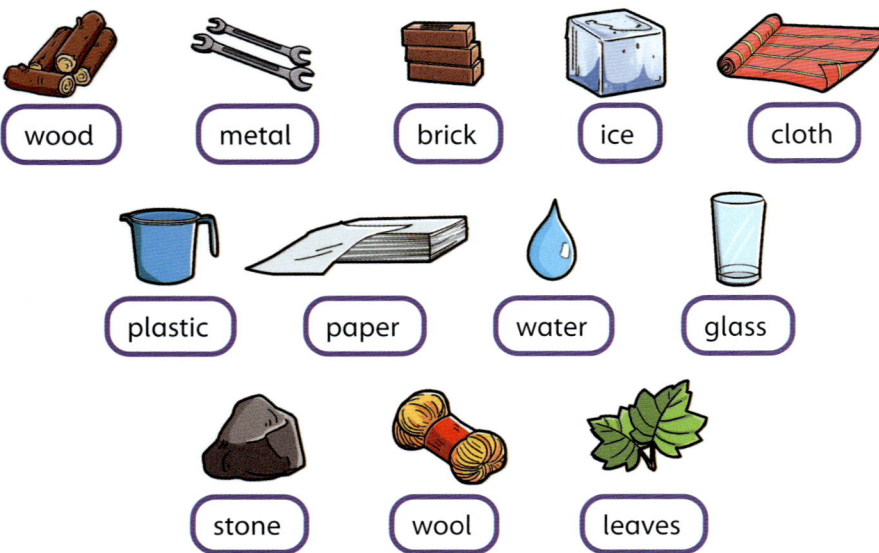

wood   metal   brick   ice   cloth

plastic   paper   water   glass

stone   wool   leaves

Classifying materials by their properties

Your teacher will give you a variety of objects to investigate.

1 Observe each object.

2 Classify them into the materials they are made from.

3 Test each material with a magnet to see if it is magnetic or non-magnetic. Agree its other properties with your partner.

4 List the name of the object, the material it is made from and two of its properties. Record your findings in a suitable table of results.

Science fact

Gold is a better electrical conductor than aluminium, but it is so expensive it is only used in smartphones and not everyday circuits. There is 1 g of gold in about 35–40 mobile phones.

Conductivity is how a material lets something pass through it. With thermal conductivity, the material lets heat pass through it. With electrical conductivity, the material lets electricity pass through it.

■ For more activities, go to Workbook 5 page 72.

Thermal conductivity is an important property for materials that are used to make cooking and heating objects, for example a cooking pan or pot. Electrical conductivity is useful when making electrical circuits.

 ## Investigating the conductivity of materials

Thermal conductivity

Your teacher will give you three spoons made from either wood, metal or plastic.

1 Predict which material will be a good thermal conductor.

2 Use a thermometer or thermometer strip. Measure and record the temperature of the end of each spoon.

3 Place the spoons in a beaker of boiling water for 1 minute.

4 Measure and record the temperature of each using the same method.

5 Which material was the best thermal conductor?

This is the one where the temperature increased the most.

6 Was your prediction correct?

7 Evaluate the method. Would you change anything?

Electrical conductivity

Your teacher will give you some materials to test. Can you remember how you used a test circuit?

1 Set up a circuit like the one in the diagram.

2 Predict which material will be a good electrical conductor.

3 Test the materials to find out if your prediction is correct.

Remember – connect the test material across the gap. If the bulb lights, the material is an electrical conductor.

4 Was your prediction correct?

 Warning!
Some of the spoons will get very hot, so be careful not to touch them.

Test circuit

Can you see a pattern in your results? Is there any link between thermal and electrical conductors?

 Stretch zone

Research new materials that have been developed in the last three years. Choose one that interests you most. Write a short report on how it was developed and why it will be useful in our world.

Key idea

Materials have properties. Their properties make some materials more useful than others.

■ For more activities, go to Workbook 5 page 73.

Reversible and irreversible changes

In this lesson you will understand the difference between a reversible and an irreversible change.

Key words
reversible/irreversible reaction

Irreversible changes

This cake has been baked. The cake mixture contained flour, cocoa, butter or oil, sugar and eggs.

When you mix chemicals together, sometimes they join together to make new chemicals.

We call this a chemical reaction.

Can you get the eggs back out of the cake?

The chemicals added to a chemical reaction are called the reactants. The new chemicals made are called the products. The reaction can be shown with an arrow.

Reactant A + Reactant B $\longrightarrow$ Product C + Product D

There are some clues to look for during a chemical reaction.

- Sometimes a gas is made. You may see gas bubbles. The gas may have a smell.
- New chemicals can be made, which may be a different colour.
- There may be a change in the temperature. Some reactions give out a lot of heat. Other reactions feel cold.

Chemical reactions make new materials. When reactions like this take place it is not possible to reverse them. The change is permanent. This is an irreversible reaction.

Steel rusting is an irreversible reaction. The rust is different from the steel.

■ For more activities, go to Workbook 5 page 74.

Reversible changes

Look at this photograph. Water has been made into ice cubes.

Can you get the water back from ice cubes?

Think back

Think about the changes of state you have seen before. What state of matter are ice, water and steam?

Changes of state such as melting, freezing and evaporation are reversible changes.

Dissolving sugar in a cup of tea is also a reversible change. The sugar may look and behave differently once it has dissolved in tea, but it is still the same chemical.

Reversible changes are also called physical changes.

Observing reversible and irreversible changes

1   Add a spoonful of salt to 100 cm³ of water in a cup. Stir the mixture and then pour it into a shallow saucer.

2   Leave the saucer on a sunny windowsill.

3   Carefully burn a small piece of paper. Place the burned paper and ash onto another shallow saucer.

4   Leave the saucer on a sunny windowsill.

5   Observe both of your saucers every ten minutes for an hour. Record any changes you see.

Warning!
Hold the paper in some tongs. Hold it over a metal or ceramic plate. What could happen if you did not do this?

What happened to the salt and water during the hour?
What happened to the burned paper during the hour?
What does this tell you about reversible and irreversible changes?

Stretch zone

How could you get the salt and the water back from a salt and water mixture? Share your ideas with the class.

Key idea

Some chemical reactions or changes can be reversed but others cannot.

■ For more activities, go to Workbook 5 page 75.

Are cooking, heating and burning reversible or irreversible changes?

In this lesson you will explore whether cooking, heating and burning are reversible or irreversible changes.

Key words

burn

chemical

cook

fuel

heat

reversible/irreversible

   reaction

Think back

Is a chemical change reversible? Explain your answer.

Are the changes shown in these photographs reversible or irreversible?

Can the food be uncooked to get the ingredients back?

Can the bubbles be collected and put back into the tablet?

When chemical reactions happen, the changes cannot be reversed. New materials are made.

Here are some examples of reversible and irreversible changes.

Reversible changes	Irreversible changes
Melting	Cooking
Freezing	Burning
Evaporation	Rusting
Mixing	Digestion
Dissolving	Using soap

Examples of reversible and irreversible changes

1   Talk about each of the changes in the table.

2   Write one example of each that you have seen or used.

3   Describe to your partner what happened during the change.

■ For more activities, go to Workbook 5 page 76.

What is burning?

Sometimes when materials are heated, they can burst into flames. This is called burning. The flame is energy released as heat and light. Burning is an irreversible process.

We burn some materials to give us energy for houses, cars and aeroplanes. The materials we use are very good at burning. They give out a lot of energy. We call these materials fuels. It is important that we use the right fuel.

The flame is used to burn off gas so the gas doesn't cause problems

How can we investigate burning?

We can observe whether fuels burn with a flame or not.

1   Look at the fuels your teacher gives you. Can you predict whether they will burn or not?

2   Copy and complete the table below. Record your predictions. Then carry out your investigation and write down your observations.

Type of fuel	Prediction – will this burn?	Observation – did it burn?
paper	yes	yes
twigs		
cardboard		

3   When you have completed your investigation look closely at your results.

Can you see a pattern? Write your answer in your notebook.

4   Write a conclusion.

Warning!

Be careful with naked flames. Do not lean over or put anything nearby. Why do you think this is important?

Be a scientist

A hypothesis is a scientific idea. Writing conclusions helps us to understand if our predictions and hypotheses were right. We ask if the results support our ideas.

▶ page 9

Stretch zone

Research how a scientist can show that carbon dioxide is made when fuels such as wood and paper burn. Share your ideas with the class.

Key idea

Heating, cooking and burning cause irreversible changes.

77

■ For more activities, go to Workbook 5 page 77.

Putting out fires

In this lesson you will explore that sometimes we need to control irreversible changes.

Key words
acid
bicarbonate of soda
carbon dioxide
combustion
fire extinguisher
fuel
oxygen

To make a fire you need three main things:

- fuel that can burn
- something to start the reaction of burning – this is sometimes called ignition
- oxygen – this is in the air all around us.

To help us remember the things needed for a fire to burn, we can arrange their names in a triangle. Each side of the triangle represents one of the three things needed for a fire. The order you put them in is not important.

Many fire extinguishers remove the heat that keeps the fire going.

Water cools the heat of the flame. The problem with water is that you can only use it on certain kinds of fire. You must use the right type of fire extinguisher for different fires. If you put water on an oil fire the water will fall to the bottom of the oil.

Carbon dioxide fire extinguishers stop oxygen getting to the flame. There are many ways to produce enough carbon dioxide to do this. Carbon dioxide is a gas. We breathe out carbon dioxide but this is not enough to put out a fire. Lots of carbon dioxide is needed to extinguish a flame.

When we blow out a candle, we do not do this with carbon dioxide. We blow the flame away from the fuel of the candle.

■ For more activities, go to Workbook 5 page 78.

We can make carbon dioxide gas. When acid is added to chalk or limestone the chalk or limestone reacts. The fizzing is carbon dioxide.

Vinegar is an acid. If we mix it with chalk, we make carbon dioxide.

 ## Make and test a fire extinguisher

Your teacher will give you acetic acid (vinegar) and bicarbonate of soda. When these chemicals react, they produce carbon dioxide gas. This is a very quick reaction so replace the lid quickly.

 Warning!
Be very careful with a flame. Do not lean over it or place things near it. Never touch the flame as it will burn you.

1 You will need to make a fire to test your fire extinguisher. Think about how you will keep safe.

2 Write down your plan before you start. Include a diagram.

Did your fire extinguisher put out the fire?
What did you remove from the fire triangle?

 ## Comparing extinguishers

1 Repeat the investigation using water as your fire extinguisher.

2 Compare the two fire extinguishers you have used.

3 Write your observations in a table.

Did one of the fire extinguishers work better than the other?

Key idea

Some fire extinguishers remove heat from the fire. Carbon dioxide fire extinguishers stop oxygen getting to the flame.

 Stretch zone

Research how people who manage large forests use their knowledge of the fire triangle to help them to reduce the risk of forest fires. Share your ideas by making an information leaflet.

■ For more activities, go to Workbook 5 page 79.

Separating mixtures of solids

In this lesson you will explore how solids can be mixed and how it is often possible to then separate them again.

Key words

magnet

mixture

separate

sieve

solid

Think back

How can you tell if something is a solid?

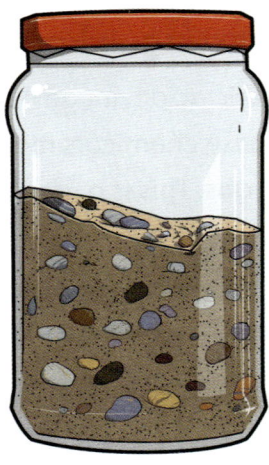

If lots of different solid things are put into a container, we call it a mixture. A mixture is made when two or more materials are placed or mixed together. The materials do not change.

Often we have to use special techniques and equipment to separate solids in a mixture.

You can use a sieve to remove the pebbles from the sand.

How could you separate the sand and pebbles in this mixture?

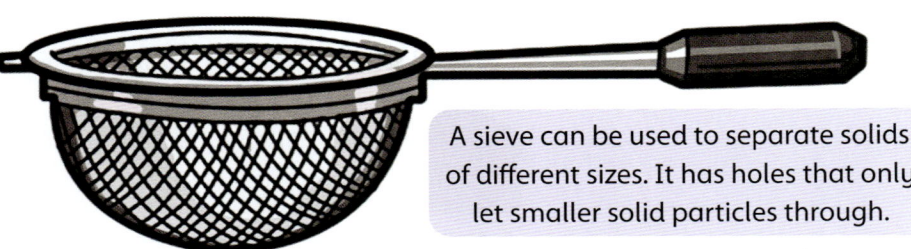

A sieve can be used to separate solids of different sizes. It has holes that only let smaller solid particles through.

Which of the sieves below would you use to separate sand from rice? Explain why.

❶

❷

❸

Be a scientist

Scientists use specialist equipment in experiments and investigations. They choose the right equipment for the job.

▶ page 9

■ For more activities, go to Workbook 5 page 80.

Gardeners use sieves to break up the soil. The stones and lumps of soil are kept in the sieve. The holes of the sieve are too small for the large particles to pass through.

Very small solids cannot be separated using a sieve. The small solids will pass through the holes.

Separating materials from different soils

A company wants to decide which of three fields to use for planting crops. They want a soil that has some sand and stones in it, so that water drains away well. However they do not want too many stones, as the plants may not grow.

The company has asked you to investigate the three different samples of soil. Each is taken from one of the fields.

1   Plan an investigation to find out how much sand and how many stones each soil sample contains.

2   Produce an information leaflet for the company to recommend one of the fields. Include a description of how you carried out the investigation, and include your results.

Talk about how to keep safe during this investigation.

Using a magnet to separate some solids from mixtures

Your teacher will give you a mixture of solids and a list of equipment. Your task is to separate some of the solids from the mixture using a magnet.

1   Look at the equipment you need.

2   Copy and complete the table below in your notebook.

Solid	Was it separated using a magnet?

3   Explain why some of the materials could be separated using a magnet but some could not.

Stretch zone

Research how magnets are used to separate parts of waste for recycling. Why is this important?

Key idea

We can use sieves and magnets to separate some solids from a mixture.

■ For more activities, go to Workbook 5 page 81.

Adding solids to water

In this lesson you will explore the changes that occur when solids are added to water.

Key words

dissolve

saturated

soluble/insoluble

solute

solution

solvent

Some solids dissolve in liquid. These are called soluble.

Some solids do not dissolve in a liquid. These are called insoluble.

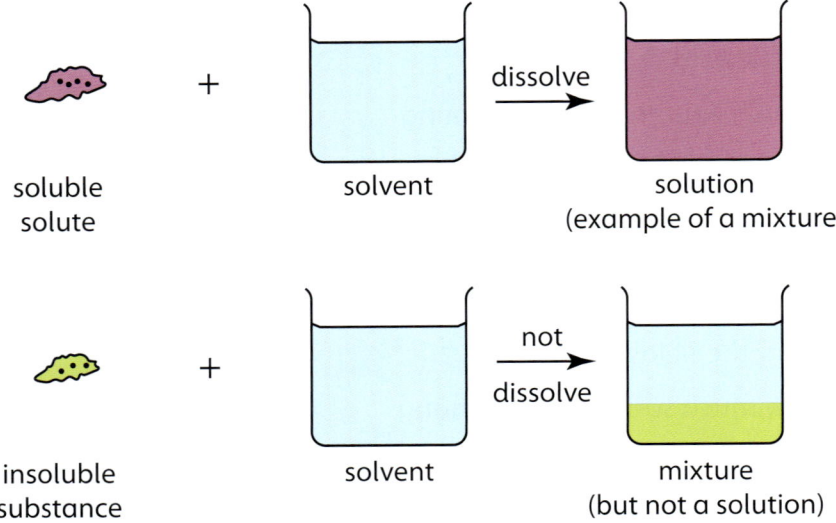

What is a soluble solid called?

What is the liquid that may or may not dissolve something called?

What do we call the mixture made when something has dissolved?

When coffee is added to water the solvent is the water. Coffee powder or granules is the solute. The cup of coffee is the solution.

When a material dissolves in a liquid it is a reversible change. You can get the material back by evaporating away the water.

How much sugar will dissolve in water?

You are going to investigate how much sugar dissolves in water.

1 How much sugar do you predict will dissolve in water?

2 You will reach a point when you cannot dissolve more sugar. What will you see? We say the solution is saturated when this happens.

3 Add 100 cm³ of water to a cup. Leave it for 10 minutes to allow it to warm up to room temperature.

4 Add one small teaspoon of sugar to the water and stir gently. Has the sugar dissolved?

5 Add another small teaspoon of sugar to the water and stir gently. Has the sugar dissolved now?

6 Keep adding sugar until no more will dissolve.

7 Record your results and observations in a suitable table.

■ For more activities, go to Workbook 5 page 82.

The ability of a material (solute) to dissolve in a liquid (solvent) is called solubility.

Does the temperature of the water affect how much sugar dissolves?

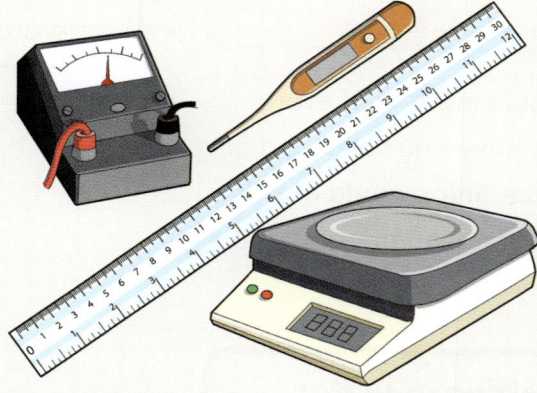

This time the temperature of the water is the independent variable. Remember: this is the thing you are changing in the investigation.

The dependent variable will be the measurement of sugar that you dissolve. This is the variable that you find out from the investigation.

Remember to identify the control variables – these are all of the things you are keeping the same.

1 Predict whether increasing the temperature of the water will increase or decrease how much sugar can dissolve. Add a hypothesis. This is the scientific explanation of your prediction.

2 Carry out the investigation and record your results.

3 Were your prediction and hypothesis correct?

4 Share your conclusions with the class by presenting your ideas to them.

Warning!
Be careful with hot water. Tell your teacher if any spills over. Why do you think this is important?

For more activities, go to Workbook 5 page 83.

Can you change the solubility of a solute?

Will the temperature of the water affect how much sugar dissolves in the water?

How can you make sure this is a fair test? Think about the amount of water you use. If you use a different amount each time will it affect the solubility?

Key ideas

- Some solids dissolve and some do not.
- Increasing the temperature of a solvent increases the amount of solute that will dissolve in it.

Stretch zone

Try to dissolve other solids and see if they are insoluble or soluble. Make a list of soluble and insoluble solids.

3 Properties and Changes of Materials

Separating insoluble solids from liquids by filtering

In this lesson you will explore how some solids that do not dissolve or react with water can be separated by filtering.

Key words
filter
filtration
insoluble
mixture
separate

Think back

What do we call a solid that does not dissolve in water? Can you name three examples?

It is very important that not everything is soluble in water. If every material dissoved in water, then we would not have any solid land or objects. Every time it rains, solids would dissolve. Ships would dissolve in the sea. Beaches and cliffs would not exist. Even solid animals and plants would dissolve!

Proving that sand does not dissolve in water

Sand does not dissolve in water. How can you prove this?

1 When you try to dissolve sand in the water what do you see?
2 Where does the sand go?

Try to stir the mixture. Does this make a difference?

Even if the water was hotter or you stirred it more, it will not dissolve. This is because sand is insoluble.

Stretch zone

Plan an investigation to show that sand will not dissolve in water, no matter how hot the water is.

Be a scientist
Scientists plan their investigations to prove their ideas. They also use secondary sources of evidence to support their ideas.
▶ page 8

Filter paper works like sieving. The holes in the paper are tiny. They stop small particles moving through the paper. This separates them from the mixture.

Filter funnel

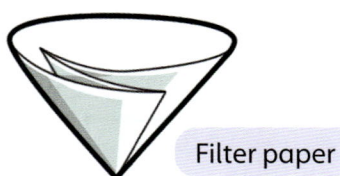
Filter paper

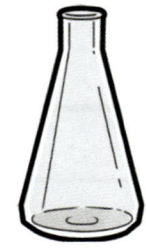
Glass flask

This process is called filtration. It is a very useful process and is used in science for separating insoluble materials from water.

■ For more activities, go to Workbook 5 page 84.

How can you separate sand from water?

1 First try pouring the water and sand mixture through a sieve. What do you observe?

2 Now try using filter paper in a filter funnel. What do you observe?

3 Which piece of equipment works the best?

Some coffee machines use filtration. Hot water is poured over the coffee very slowly. The small particles of coffee flavour the water. The bigger particles are collected in the paper.

On a much larger scale, filter beds are used to make clean water that is safe to drink.

Water filter beds

Make your own filter bed

You are going to design, make and test your own filter bed.

1 Use the diagram to help you. Think about how you could make layers of sand and carbon to act as a filter.

2 Carbon can be made by burning wood – it is charcoal. Make a list of other materials that can act as a filter.

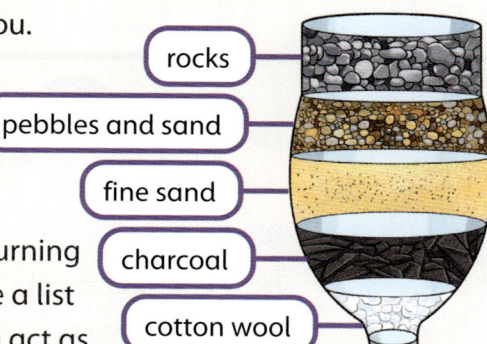

rocks

pebbles and sand

fine sand

charcoal

cotton wool

3 Pour some dirty water through your filter. How clean did it look after filtering?

Warning! Never drink water you have filtered in this way. It may look clean but could have dangerous chemicals or microorganisms in it.

4 Present your model to the class.

Compare the different models. What could you do to your filter to improve it?

3 Properties and Changes of Materials

■ For more activities, go to Workbook 5 page 85.

Using more separating techniques

In this lesson you will investigate how materials can be separated from solutions using different techniques.

Key words

chromatography

dissolve

mixture

solid

solution

Is this seawater a mixture or a pure material? Explain your answer.

Talk about two other materials you may find in seawater.

Sometimes it is easy to see whether something is a mixture or not. Sometimes it is more difficult.

Identifying mixtures

You have four materials. Two of the materials are pure. The other two are mixtures. Plan an investigation to find out which is which.

Use the discussion questions to help you.

Discuss two ways to separate mixtures.

How can you check to see whether a liquid has anything dissolved in it?

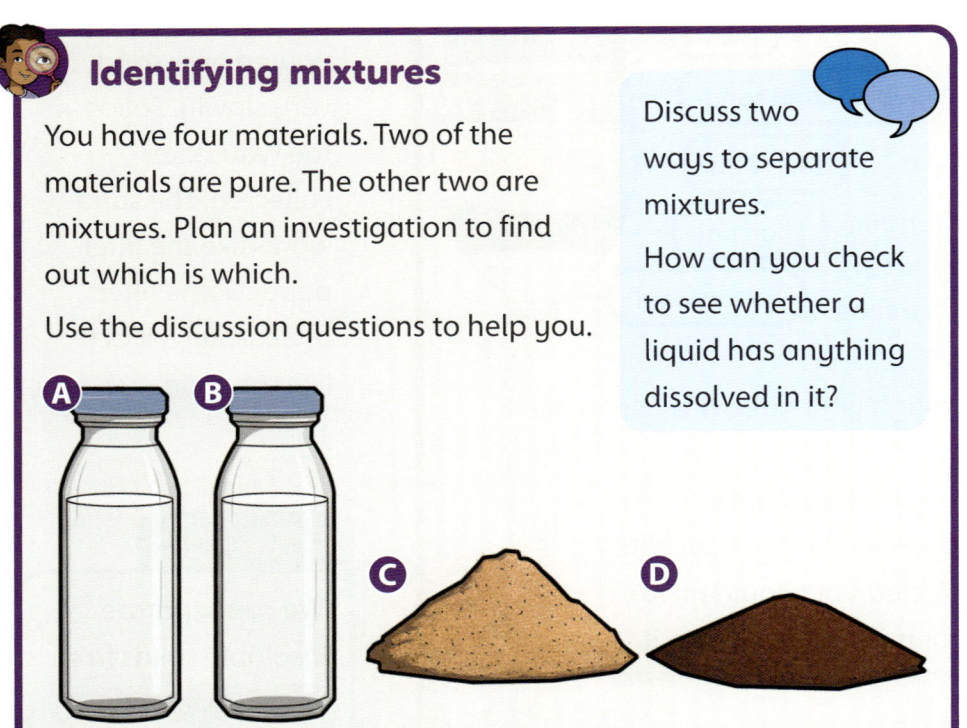

Can we separate mixtures of inks?

Chromatography is another way of separating mixtures. You can see how it works by using it to separate a mixture of coloured inks.

Science fact

Forensic scientists use chromatography to match dyes in different samples found at the scene of a crime.

■ For more activities, go to Workbook 5 page 86.

Investigating coloured inks

Plan and carry out an investigation to find out which colours are found in pen ink. Use chromatography as your technique.

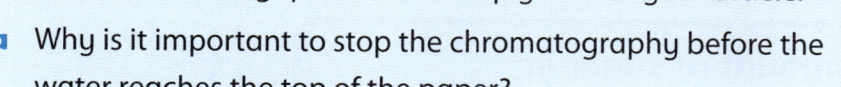

pencil

strip of paper

distance the spot of ink travelled along the paper

water

1   Place a spot of the ink near the bottom of a piece of filter paper and allow it to dry.

2   Add a small amount of water to a jar.

3   Fix the paper to a pencil and let it down into the jar so the bottom edge of the paper is dipping into the water.

4   Observe the water slowly rising up the paper and carrying some of the ink with it.

5   You must stop the experiment before the water runs all the way to the top of the paper. If it does, the ink will travel too far.

6   Investigate different coloured pens to compare the colours.

7   Write a magazine article to tell people how you separate colours from inks.

Answer the following questions to help you with your article.

a   Why is it important to stop the chromatography before the water reaches the top of the paper?

b   Why is it important that the inks dissolve in water?

c   Why can't we use chromatography to separate different coloured pencils?

Stretch zone

Scientists use chromatography to help them to develop vaccines to fight diseases. Do some research and write a short report on vaccines that were developed in this way.

Key idea

Some materials can be separated from solutions using different techniques, such as filtering and chromatography.

■ For more activities, go to Workbook 5 page 87.

Investigating solids and solutions

In this lesson you will find out how some solids dissolve in water to form solutions and understand that the material is in the solution.

Think back

Write down two times you dissolved something today or someone dissolved something for you.

When a solid dissolves in water, what is made?
Mixtures can be made if the solid does not dissolve.

Sugar is dissolved in many drinks. Drinking sugar-filled drinks is bad for your health. The sugar can cause tooth decay and you can become overweight if you have too much sugar.

Can you tell how much sugar there is in a drink just by looking at it? Explain your answer.

The liquid in a sugary drink is mainly water. This water can evaporate to form water vapour. The water vapour will rise into the air and leave any solids behind. The change from liquid water to water vapour is an example of a change of state. A liquid is changing into a gas.

Investigating the amount of sugar in sugary drinks

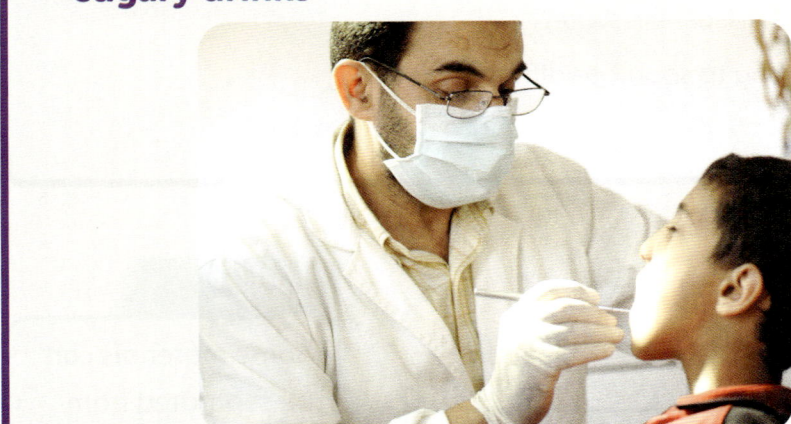

A dentist asks you to investigate some drinks. The results from your investigation will help people make the right decision about which drinks they buy.

 Warning!
Do not taste the drinks. They might not have been made with clean equipment or water.

■ For more activities, go to Workbook 5 page 88.

When you receive your samples of drinks you must plan and carry out an investigation to test how much sugar is in each of the drinks.

Some of the drinks samples look clear. This doesn't mean they do not have any sugar in them.

1   Answer the following questions to help you plan your investigation.

   a   What method will you use to separate any sugar that may be in the drink?

   b   Make a list of all the equipment you will need.

   c   How will you make this a fair test? What will you need to keep the same?

   d   How will you plan to collect reliable data?

2   Make a table of results so that you can record your findings. Which column will the independent variable go in?

3   How can you measure how much sugar there is in the drink? What pieces of equipment can you use?

4   It is difficult to see patterns in results when they are in a table. Drawing graphs and charts makes it much easier to see patterns.

   Draw a bar chart in your notebook to show how much sugar there is in the drinks you have tested.

5   Look at your results. Can you write a conclusion?

Separating the sugar from the drink using evaporation shows that dissolving is a reversible change.

Stretch zone

Plan an investigation to separate water from a sugary drink – but this time you want to collect the water. Think about changes of state.

■ For more activities, go to Workbook 5 page 89.

Be a scientist

If you plan a fair test this means other scientists can repeat the investigation. You can then compare lots of results. This means the results will be more reliable.

▶ page 9

Did any of the drinks not have any sugar in them? These are the ones you can recommend to the dentist. If they all had sugar the one with the lowest amount is better for you.

Key idea

Although a solid in solution cannot be seen, the material is still present and can be separated from the solution again.

3 Properties and Changes of Materials

Energy changes and reactions

In this lesson you will explore the energy changes that occur in some reactions.

Key words

energy

exothermic

heat

reactants

reaction

temperature

Think back

Can you remember the changes that can happen in a chemical reaction?

Reactions happen when we mix chemicals together. The chemicals we add to a reaction are called the reactants.

The reactants join together and make new materials. It is not possible to reverse this kind of reaction.

When you burn a piece of magnesium ribbon, the magnesium combines with the oxygen in the air and the product is magnesium oxide. This is an irreversible reaction.

The reaction releases lots of energy. It needs heat to start the reaction and then the reactants release energy. The flame burns so brightly that it is dangerous to look at it directly.

Plaster of Paris is used for lots of things. It is sometimes used to make casts to help people's broken bones to repair. Some people use it to make models and statues. It is also used in tablets that you take when you are ill.

Look at the pictures below. The plaster of Paris is being mixed with the water to produce a smooth paste.

What happens to the temperature in a reaction?

The temperature increases as the reactants are mixed together. This is called an exothermic reaction. The chemicals produce their own heat.

If you break up the word 'exothermic' into 'exo' and 'therm' does it become clearer?

- 'exo' comes from the Greek word meaning outside
- 'therm' comes from thermal which means heat

So exothermic means heat outside. Heat goes outside or leaves the reaction.

Burning magnesium

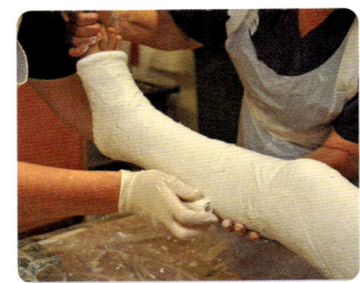

Cast on a broken leg

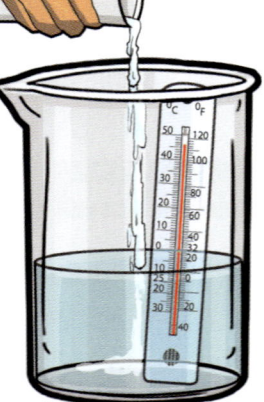

■ For more activities, go to Workbook 5 page 90.

Burning or combustion is also an exothermic reaction. We know this because it releases heat. We use this heat to cook food and warm our homes.

Concrete is a very common building material. It is made by mixing small rocks, sand, cement and water. These react together and, when they set, a very hard material is produced.

 Is the process of making concrete an exothermic reaction?

Your teacher will make a mixture of small stones, sand and cement.

1 The water will be in a bowl. Find the temperature of the water before it is added to the mixture of small stones, sand and cement.

2 Your teacher will now add the water to the mix and stir it gently. Record the temperature of the concrete mix after the water is added.

3 Write a science report to tell people about the temperature change when concrete is made.

4 To help you to write up your investigation, discuss the questions below.

   a What do you notice about the change in temperature?

   b Do you think this reaction is reversible?

   c Is this reaction exothermic? Explain your answer.

 Warning!
Cement powder can burn your hands and eyes. Wear protective gloves and eye glasses when you are near to the mixture.

Be a scientist
Scientists use equipment such as thermometers very carefully to obtain accurate results. They often repeat their readings to check results.

▶ page 10

Discuss all the uses of concrete you know. Look around the room you are in, or outside.

 Stretch zone

Imagine that chemical reactions never give out heat. What will happen to cooking stoves, fireworks, matches, cars, trains and electricity? How will your world change? Tell your partner.

Check how much you know.

Try the questions on pages 92–93.

Key idea
Some reactions give out heat. They are called exothermic reactions.

■ For more activities, go to Workbook 5 page 91.

1 Tick the examples of reversible reactions.

2 Circle the correct words.

   a A solid that dissolves in water is called a: solute   solution   solvent

   b A liquid that dissolves a solid is called a: solute   solution   solvent

   c A mixture when something dissolves in water is called a: solute   solution   solvent

3 Draw a line between each image and the correct word box to show whether they are soluble or insoluble.

chalk   sawdust   sugar

sand   salt

soluble   insoluble

4 Label the diagram to show the three things needed for a fire to burn. Use the words in the word box to help you.

oxygen   ignition   fuel

■ For more activities, go to Workbook 5 page 92.

5 Write the process you could use to separate these mixtures:

a sand and water _____

b salt and water _____

c sand and pebbles _____

6 Describe a way to make a soluble material dissolve more quickly in water.

_____

7 **a** Label the diagram.

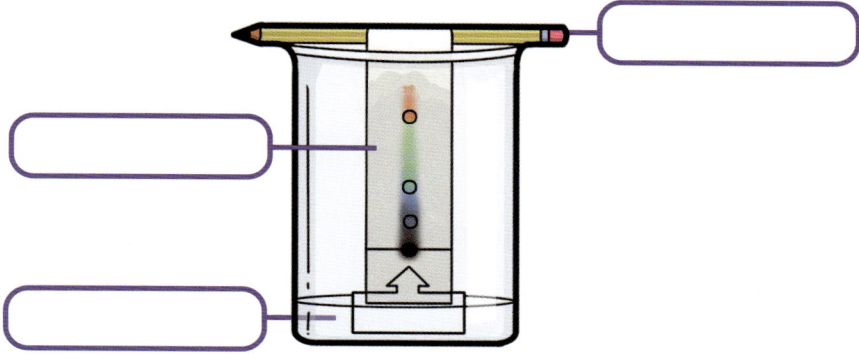

b What is this separation technique called? _____

c Give one use of this technique.

_____

8 Study the table below. It shows how much sugar was found in different sugary drinks.

Sugary drink	Number of grams of sugar in 100 cm³ of drink
A	5
B	3
C	8
D	2

a Explain how the water could be removed from the sugary drink to leave the sugar.

_____

b Why was 100 cm³ of sugary drink used each time?

_____

c Which drink has the most sugar dissolved in it? _____

d Which drink has the least sugar dissolved in it? _____

■ For more activities, go to Workbook 5 page 93.

3 Properties and Changes of Materials

In this unit you will:

- describe the movement of the Earth and other planets in the solar system
- describe the movement of the Moon around the Earth
- explore that the Sun does not move; it appears to move because of how the Earth spins on its axis
- discover that the Earth spins on its axis once every 24 hours
- explore the changing size and position of shadows throughout the day
- discover that the Earth takes a year to orbit the Sun, spinning as it goes
- learn that the Sun, Earth and Moon are shaped like spheres.

axis   day   Earth
Moon   night   orbit
planet   rotate   shadow
solar system   sphere
star   Sun   year

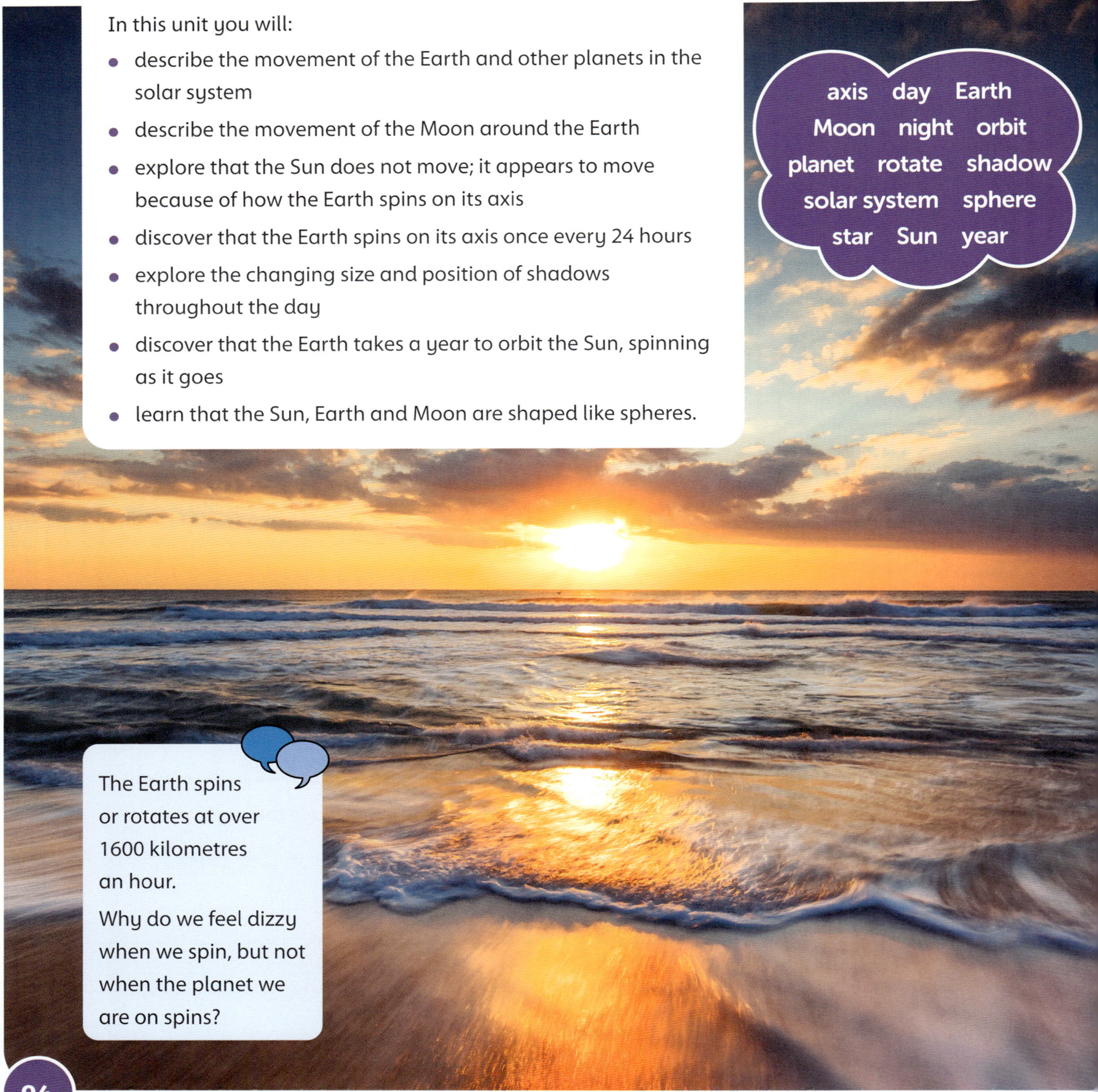

The Earth spins or rotates at over 1600 kilometres an hour.

Why do we feel dizzy when we spin, but not when the planet we are on spins?

THE SUN IS FALLING OUT OF THE SKY LATER TODAY!

Some people think that the Sun moves across the sky every day.

What do you think?

Science fact

Some stars are so far away that it takes time for the light to reach our eyes. When we see the Moon, we are seeing it as it was one second ago. When we see the Sun, we are seeing it as it was about eight minutes ago.

Some planets are so far away that if people on that planet were looking at us now, they would see the pyramids being built!

■ For more activities, go to Workbook 5 pages 94–95.

The solar system

In this lesson you will explore the solar system.

Neptune
Saturn
Mars
Venus
Uranus
Jupiter
Earth
Mercury
Sun

A model of our solar system

Key words

Earth
galaxy
orbit
planet
solar system
Sun

The solar system is the Sun and everything that travels around it. The Sun is at the centre and it has eight planets. The planets travel around the Sun. The paths they take are called orbits.

Hundreds of years ago, scientists thought that the Earth was at the centre of the solar system. They could not explain why the Sun seemed to move across the sky.

Four hundred years ago an astronomer named Galileo built a telescope. He could then see the Moon, planets and stars more clearly. Galileo proved that the Sun was at the centre of the solar system.

Which four planets are closest to the Sun? Close the book. In a group of 8, label each person as a planet and stand in the correct order from the Sun.

Modelling our solar system

You are going to work in groups to make a scaled model of the planets of our solar system. A scaled model is smaller than the original but represents the sizes and distances. You will use a line constructed in your classroom to place the planets in the correct order.

1   Your teacher will give each group a planet or our Moon to create.

2   Using circular card, cut out a scaled model of your planet or our Moon. Colour it in the right colours.

3   Hang your model on the line in the correct place in relation to the Sun.

Science fact

Scientists have used telescopes and space probes to discover that planetary systems such as the solar system contain stars and planets, but also large rocks called asteroids and icy comets.

■ For more activities, go to Workbook 5 page 96.

It is important to know that when we look at planets in the night sky they do not make their own light. They are reflecting light from the Sun. So far, there is no sign of life on any planet other than the Earth.

Planet	Distance from the Sun (million km)	Mean surface temperature (°C)
Mercury	58	170
Venus	108	460
Earth	150	15
Mars	228	−50
Jupiter	778	−143
Saturn	1427	−195
Uranus	2870	−201
Neptune	4497	−220

Look at the data in the table.

Why do you think there might not be life on any other planet?

Telescopes are now much more efficient than Galileo's telescope. The Hubble telescope can see a distance of several billion light years. Space travel has also provided evidence that the Earth is spherical. You will learn more about this later. There are hundreds of images and video clips of the Earth from space.

Hubble telescope

Stretch zone

Pluto was part of the solar system until 2006. Use the internet to write a short report on why it is now classed as a 'dwarf' planet.

Key idea

The Sun is at the centre of our solar system and it has eight planets that orbit it.

■ For more activities, go to Workbook 5 page 97.

The Sun appears to move, but it doesn't

In this lesson you will explore the movement of the Earth around the Sun, and the Moon around the Earth.

Key words

axis

celestial bodies

Earth

Moon

orbit

planet

satellite

star

Think back

Can you remember the planets in our solar system?

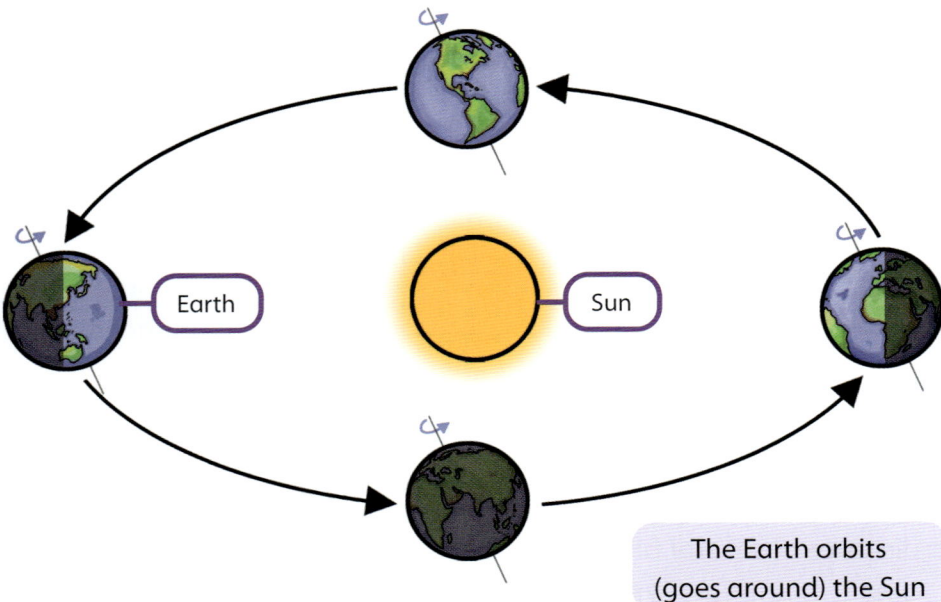

Earth

Sun

The Earth orbits (goes around) the Sun

The Sun is a star. A star produces its own light. Planets do not produce their own light. We can see them because they reflect the Sun's light.

The Sun is in the middle of the solar system. The Earth and the other planets of the solar system orbit the Sun.

The heat and light the Sun gives the Earth make it perfect for life.

The Moon is not a planet. It is a satellite of the Earth. A satellite is an object that orbits another object. The Moon is much smaller than the Sun and the Earth. We could fit almost four Moons into the Earth. Other planets have moons as well. For example, Jupiter has four large moons and many smaller ones. Moons are examples of celestial bodies. These are any objects, including moons and planets, that are outside the Earth's atmosphere.

Recap these points:

- What is the difference between a star and a planet?
- Is the Moon a planet or a satellite?
- How does the Earth's distance from the Sun allow life to survive?

98

■ For more activities, go to Workbook 5 page 98.

It is very difficult to imagine the sizes of stars and planets because they are so big. Sometimes scientists model things that they cannot see clearly, for example:

- the Moon could be shown as a bead
- the Earth could be shown as a tennis ball
- the Sun could be shown as a football.

Why do some people think that the Sun moves?

You might have heard people say that the Sun rises in the east and sets in the west. This makes you think that the Sun is moving. The Sun does not move. It is really the Earth spinning on its own axis.

An axis is an imaginary line through the Earth. It is like pushing a stick through a tennis ball. At one end of the axis there is the North Pole and at the other end there is the South Pole.

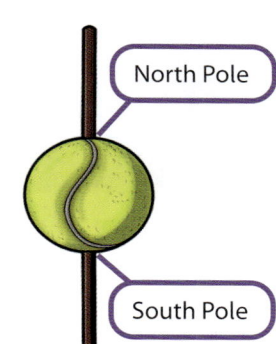

North Pole

South Pole

The Earth spins on its axis but that is not the only movement it makes.

The Earth also moves around the Sun. The path of the Earth around the Sun is called its orbit. All of the planets in our solar system orbit the Sun. The Moon orbits the Earth.

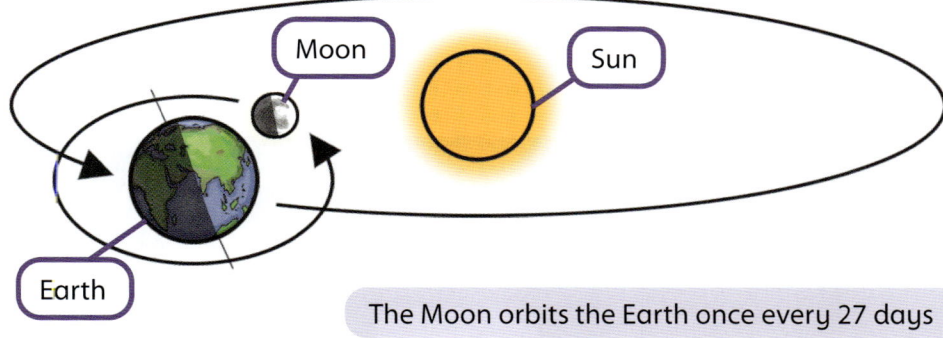

Moon

Sun

Earth

The Moon orbits the Earth once every 27 days

Key ideas

- The Earth spins and moves through space around the Sun.
- The Moon is a satellite and moves around the Earth.

Stretch zone

Research and draw how the Moon looks from Earth over a month. Make a poster and call it 'The phases of the Moon'.

4 Earth and Space

■ For more activities, go to Workbook 5 page 99.

Day and night

In this lesson you will explore how the Earth spinning on its axis gives us day and night.

Think back

Why is it not daylight all day and all night? How does this link to what the Sun appears to do?

Key words

day/night
shadow
spin

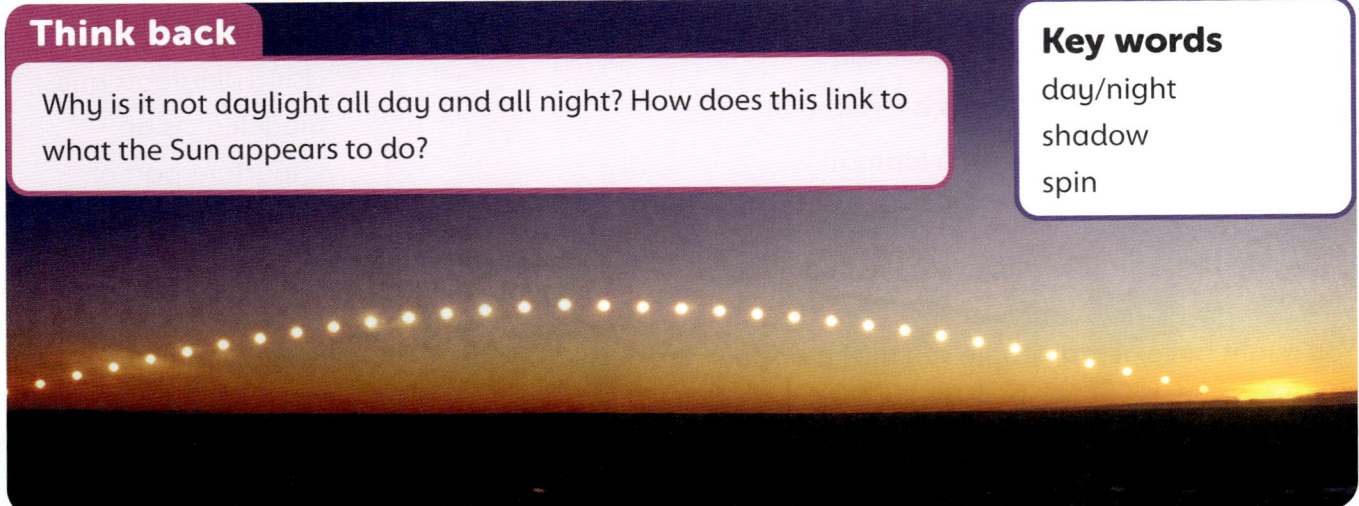

The Sun seems to move from one side of the Earth to the other.

The apparent movement of the Sun can be captured on film and in photographs. It is hard to believe that the Sun isn't moving in the solar system. It is fixed in the middle.

It is actually the Earth spinning on its axis that makes it look like the Sun is moving. The Earth makes a complete turn every 24 hours. We call this a day.

At any time, one half of the Earth is in shadow and the other half is lit by the Sun. We have daytime when the place where we live is turned towards the Sun. We have night-time when the place where we live is turned away from the Sun. We get daytime and night-time in each 24-hour period.

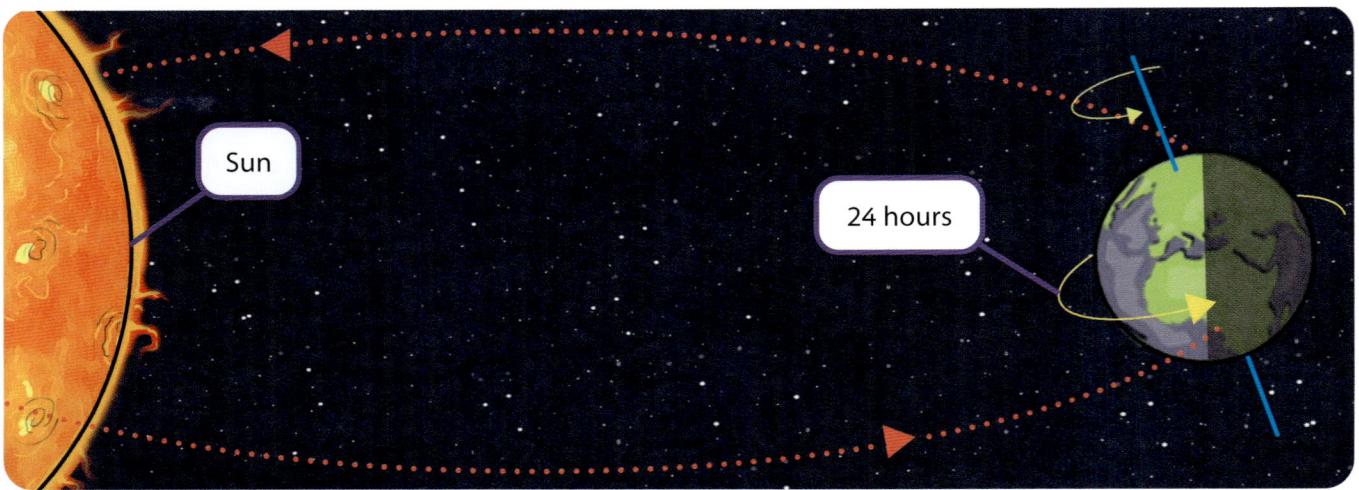

Sun

24 hours

■ For more activities, go to Workbook 5 page 100.

Where is the Sun shining in your classroom?

Your teacher will give you a simple diagram of your classroom clearly showing the windows.

Warning!

Do not look directly at the Sun, even wearing dark glasses. Discuss why this is important.

1   Mark on your diagram which window the Sun is shining through. Write the time of day on the diagram.

2   Keep a record of where the Sun is shining every 30 minutes for the rest of the school day. Number the windows and record your results in a table like the one shown below.

3   Record your observations of the Sun. Think about the following questions to help you:
   - Can you feel the heat from the Sun?
   - How far does the light shine into the room?

Window	Time of day	Observations
1		
2		

4   Look at your diagram and table of results. What do you notice? Does the sunlight come through different windows at different times of the day?

5   Can you use your table of results to predict the time?

   You could test this prediction on the following days after the investigation. Look at the window the Sun is shining through. Now look at your results. At what time did it shine through that window in your investigation? Check to see if it is the same time.

Is this a reliable way to tell the time?

Explain why your results might not be reliable.

What can you do to make sure you collect reliable results?

Be a scientist

Sometimes, scientists compare their results with other people's. This is to make sure their results are reliable. The results they collect from other people are called secondary data. Remember, the more results you collect that fit the same pattern, the more reliable the results are.

▶ page 8

How can you use secondary data here?

6   Repeat this investigation over the next few weeks.

The position of the Sun can help us to work out the time of day.

Key idea

The Earth spins on its axis once in every 24 hours. This makes night and day.

■ For more activities, go to Workbook 5 page 101.

4 Earth and Space

How long does it take the Earth to spin on its axis?

In this lesson you will explore that the Earth spins on its own axis once in every 24 hours, and this period includes daytime and night-time.

Key words

axis
Earth
rotate
spin
tilt

Think back

How many hours are there in a day? Remember that in scientific terms, a day is a period of night and day.

The Earth spins at speeds above 1600 kilometres an hour. We do not feel this because everything else on the Earth is spinning at the same speed.

Although the Earth is spinning at such a high speed, it still takes 24 hours for it to make a complete spin. The time it takes the Earth to make one full spin is how we measure a day. This period includes daytime and night-time.

Think about all of the things you do in a day. Remember night-time as well. How do you know that it is morning? What sounds do you hear? What can you smell? How much sunlight is there? Then, how do you know that it is the end of the day?

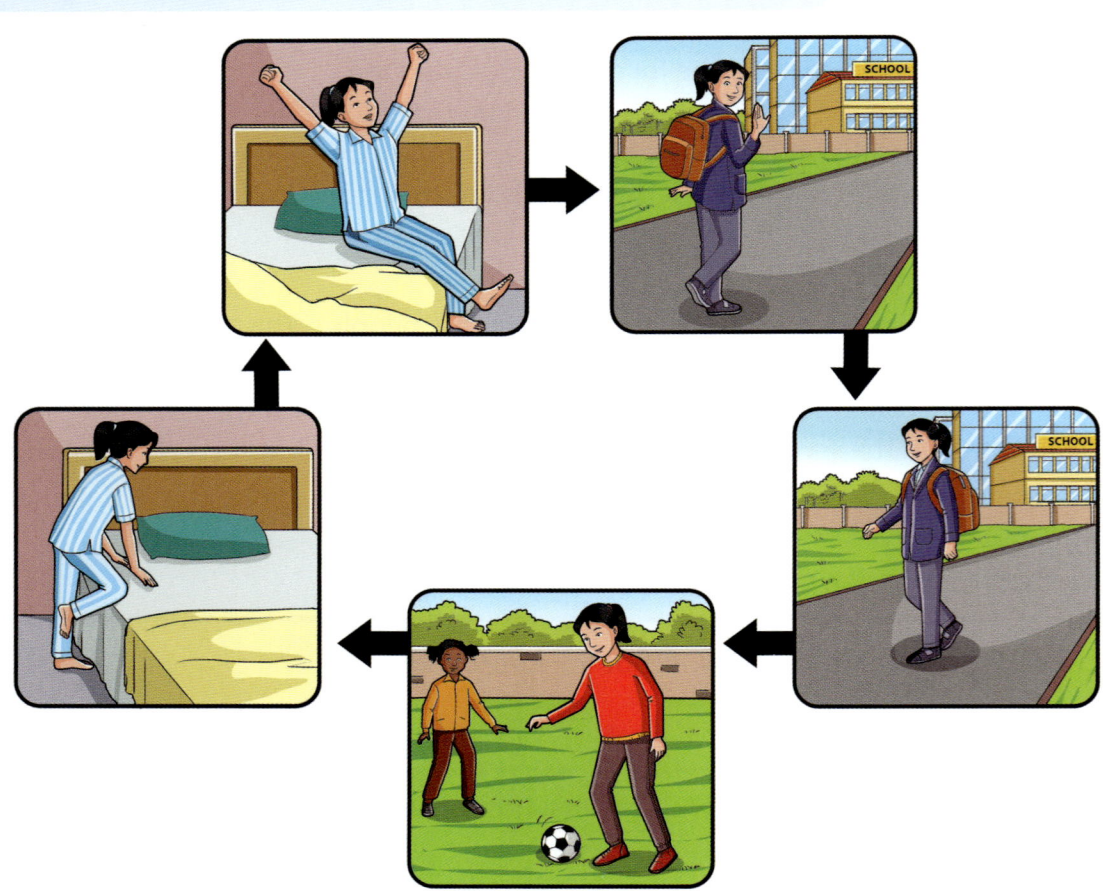

■ For more activities, go to Workbook 5 page 102.

Look at the diagram. Notice that the axis is slightly tilted. The blue arrow shows the direction of the Earth's spin. Certain parts of the Earth are in darkness for some of the time. This is because that part of the Earth is no longer facing the Sun. This is night-time on those parts of the Earth.

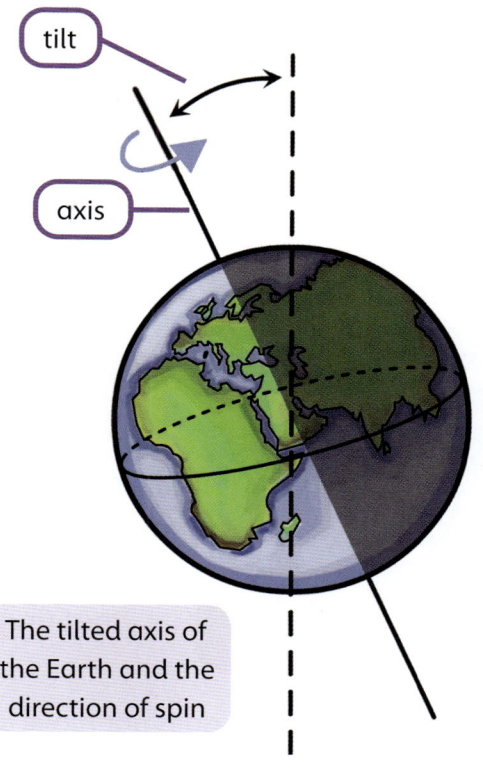

tilt

axis

The tilted axis of the Earth and the direction of spin

Modelling the Earth's spin

1 Make a model of the Earth using modelling clay.

2 Make an axis with a stick or a pencil.

3 Ask your partner to hold a lit torch in position. The torch is a model of the Sun.

4 Put a tiny ball of clay on the surface of your Earth. This is you. Hold your Earth in front of the Sun and carefully spin it.

What happens to the sunlight on you?

Are you in sunlight for a whole spin?

Warning! Take care when pushing the stick through the centre of your modelling clay. Why do you think this is important?

Stretch zone

Research the other planets in the solar system and find out how long it takes them to rotate (spin) on their axis (the length of an Earth day) and how long it takes them to orbit the Sun (an Earth year). Present your findings in a table.

Key idea

The Earth spins once every 24 hours or one day. It is night-time in the parts of the Earth that face away from the Sun.

■ For more activities, go to Workbook 5 page 103.

Shadows move and change

In this lesson you will explore the changing size and position of shadows throughout the day.

Key words

axis

Earth

horizon

shadow

Sun

Think back

Why does the direction and length of shadows change during the day?

To stay cool in the Sun, we can sit in the shadow of a tree or a sunshade. If we stay there all day, we will have to move to stay out of the Sun. Why?

As you have explored, the Sun does not move across the sky. It is the Earth that is spinning on its axis that gives the impression that the Sun is moving.

Measuring the length and position of a shadow to show the apparent movement of the Sun

You are going to carry out an investigation on the Sun using shadows.

1 Find a flat, clean and safe space outside. Sit on the floor and observe the length and width of your shadow.

2 Stand up and ask your partner to draw around your shadow. Swap roles so that your partner stands up and you draw around their shadow. Measure the length and width of your shadows.

3 Take it in turns to lie down next to your drawn shadow. Ask your partner to compare you with your drawn shadow. Record your results in a table like the one shown.

Time of day	Length of shadow (cm)	Width of shadow (cm)	Height of the Sun (cm)	Observations

Is your shadow smaller or bigger than you?

How does the shape of your shadow change?

Is there a link between the size of the shadow and the height of the Sun?

104

4   To observe the apparent movement of the Sun, scientists sometimes measure how high the Sun is in the sky. Sit on the ground with the Sun in front of you.

5   Hold up a ruler so that the bottom is level with the horizon. Cover the Sun with your thumb. Looking out of the corner of your eye, estimate the height of the Sun using the ruler. Record your results in the same table. You could repeat this investigation at different times during the day.

This girl is looking out of the corner of her eye

Warning! Never look directly at the Sun. It will damage your eyesight.

Does the position of your shadow move throughout the day?

The Earth is spinning, making the Sun appear to change position. What affect does this have on the position of your shadow throughout the day?

1   Go outside. Find a large space. Ask your partner to stand in front of the Sun. Mark the position of their feet on the floor. Use a piece of chalk or a sticker. Now draw around the shadow formed by their body.

2   Repeat this at lunchtime and just before you go home. You could take a photograph of the drawings on the floor.

Has the position of the shadow moved on the floor? Why? Your partner did not move.

Key idea

The spinning of the Earth results in shadows changing size and position during the day.

The Earth spinning causes its position in front of the Sun to change. This has made the shadow move.

■ For more activities, go to Workbook 5 page 105.

We say the Sun rises and sets

In this lesson you will explore the apparent movement of the Sun during the day.

You will have noticed that the Sun appears to rise in the morning to mark the end of night and the beginning of day. This is called sunrise.

The Sun then appears to go down in the evening to mark the end of day and the beginning of night. This is called sunset.

Day and night happen at different times across the world. Even where you live, the Sun rises and sets at different times during the year.

Talk about the length of days where you live. Do they change over the year or do they stay the same?

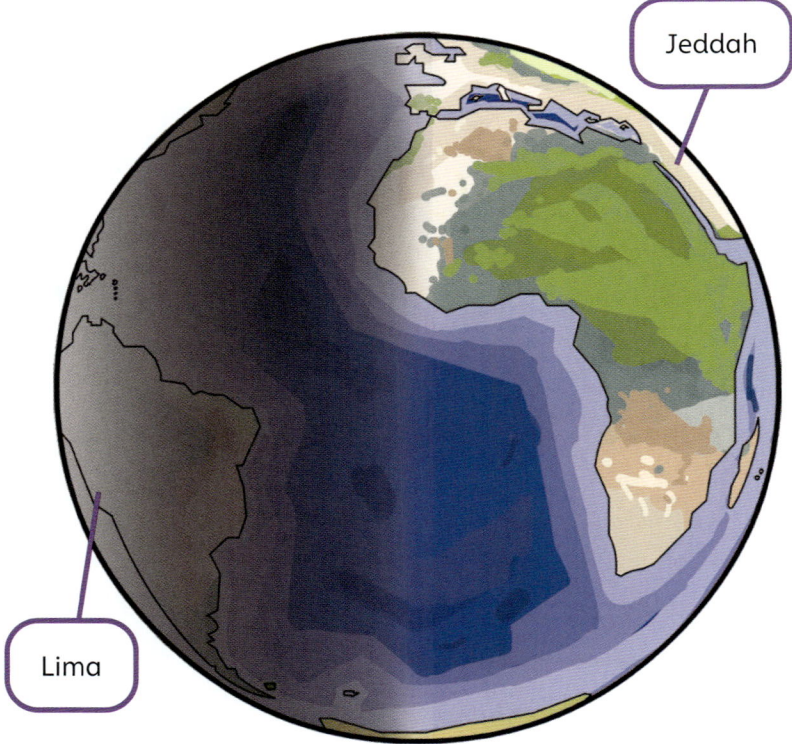

Jeddah

Lima

When it is daytime in Jeddah it is night-time in Lima

Science fact

Near the poles of the Earth it can be daylight for six months and night-time for six months.

■ For more activities, go to Workbook 5 page 106.

Look at the table below. On 1 March 2013, the sunrise time in Jeddah, Saudi Arabia was at 06.44. The sunset time was 18.28. The total amount of sunlight on that day was 11 hours, 43 minutes and 28 seconds.

On 31 March 2013, the sunrise time was 06.17. The sunset time was 18.38. The total amount of sunlight was 12 hours, 20 minutes and 32 seconds.

Which day had the most sunlight?

Month	Sunrise time	Sunset time	Total hours of sunlight
January	07.01	17.53	10h 52m
February	07.00	18.13	11h 13m
March	06.44	18.28	11h 44m
April	06.16	18.38	12h 22m
May	05.52	18.49	12h 57m
June	05.40	19.02	13h 22m
July	05.44	19.09	13h 25m
August	05.56	19.02	13h 06m
September	06.07	18.40	12h 33m
October	06.15	18.11	11h 56m
November	06.27	17.46	11h 19m
December	06.45	17.39	10h 54m

Average sunrise and sunset times for Jeddah in Saudi Arabia in 2013

Describe the pattern in the data. Do some months have more sunlight hours than others?

Be a scientist

Scientists use graphs to display results and show patterns in data. This also allows them to compare different data.

▶ page 11

It is difficult to read big tables of results like this. It would be easier to see patterns on a graph.

What kind of graph could you draw? The independent variable is the month of the year.

Stretch zone

Are all sunlight hours in a day the same length in countries a) far north of the equator, b) near the equator, and c) far south of the equator? Write a report to share your ideas.

Key ideas

- The Sun appears to rise and set every day.
- Sunrise and sunset times are different in different places around the world.

■ For more activities, go to Workbook 5 page 107.

The seasons in a year

In this lesson you will discover that the Earth takes a year to orbit the Sun, spinning as it goes.

Key words

Earth
equator
gravity
orbit
season
Sun
tilt
year

You may recall that the Earth's axis is tilted. This means that when the Earth's axis points towards the Sun, the places in that half of the Earth have summer. When the Earth's axis points away from the Sun, the places in that part of the Earth have winter.

Over a year many places have summer and winter and the seasons between them – spring and autumn (also called fall).

Look outside. How has the view changed over the past year? Have any of the buildings changed? How have any trees or plants changed?

Look at the photographs. What changes might happen over the year?

Countries near the equator have climates that do not change much over a year because they are never tilted too far away from the Sun. Further north and south, countries can have warm summers and cold, icy winters.

While the Earth is spinning on its own axis, it is also orbiting the Sun. The Earth is held in orbit by the Sun's gravity.

The Earth continuously travels around the Sun, spinning as it goes. It takes $365\frac{1}{4}$ days to do this. $365\frac{1}{4}$ days is one full year.

Remember that a day is one complete spin of the Earth, so there are $365\frac{1}{4}$ spins in a year.

What happens to the quarter of a day? We don't have a shorter day every year!

The tilted axis of the Earth and the direction of spin

Every four years we have a 'leap year'. We add up all the quarters of a day and make them into an extra day in February.

■ For more activities, go to Workbook 5 page 108.

Look at the diagram on the previous page. When the Earth is facing the Sun some parts are closer to the Sun than others. This gives us the seasons of the year.

Modelling the movements of the Earth

1   Working in pairs, ask your partner to stand very still in a space holding a lit torch. They are the Sun.

2   Stand opposite your partner and hold a large ball. Tilt it on its axis and turn it in an anticlockwise direction. You are the Earth.

3   Now try to orbit the Sun in an anticlockwise direction at the same time as spinning anticlockwise on your axis. You are modelling a day as you spin and a year as you orbit.

4   Record which parts of the ball are in light and dark. You could draw or photograph it.

5   Keep the ball tilted on its axis and move around the orbit. Record the light and dark when you are a quarter, half and three-quarters of the way around the orbit.

6   Take turns to be the Sun and the Earth.

7   Present your model to the class. Tell them when it is spring, summer, autumn and winter in the northern hemisphere of your model Earth.

Other planets in our solar system do not have $365\frac{1}{4}$ days in their year.

The length of a year on other planets is compared with the length of a year on Earth. This is an Earth Year. For example, a year on Saturn is 29 times longer than a year on Earth. It takes Neptune 165 Earth years to orbit the Sun. That is a long time between birthdays!

Planet	Length of year
Mars	2 Earth years
Jupiter	12 Earth years
Saturn	29 Earth years
Uranus	84 Earth years
Neptune	165 Earth years

Stretch zone

How would you measure your age if you lived on Neptune?

Find out how many days make a year on Mercury and Venus.

Key idea

The Earth takes $365\frac{1}{4}$ days, or a year, to orbit the Sun. Every four years we have a leap year to account for the quarter days.

■ For more activities, go to Workbook 5 page 109.

The shape of the Earth, Sun and Moon

In this lesson you will explore the evidence about the shape of the Earth, Sun and Moon.

Key words

evidence

reliable

sphere

People have studied the stars and planets for over 6000 years. These people are called cosmologists. They made models of the positions and movements of the planets and stars. They knew lots of facts about the planets, but many thought that the Earth was flat. They did not have any evidence to question it.

Aristotle was born about 2500 years ago. He had a very interesting job. He was a thinker! He thought that the world was not flat but spherical. He tried to get other people to believe this. Eventually most people agreed.

What shape do you think the Earth is? What evidence do you have?

People once believed that the Sun and planets orbited the Earth and that the Earth was the centre of the solar system. This is known as the geocentric (Earth-centred) model.

Scientists such as Ptolomy, Alhazan and Copernicus suggested that the Sun is the centre of the solar system. This is known as the heliocentric (Sun-centred) model.

Stretch zone

Research the work of Ptolomy, Alhazan and Copernicus. Write down when they lived and what they observed and found out.

Aristotle

110

In the 19th century, an English inventor called Samuel Rowbotham decided that the Earth was flat after all. He set up a society, or group, to try to convince everyone that the Earth was flat.

How do scientists prove they are right?

Samuel carried out tests but he did not know that his experiments were wrong, so his results were also wrong. Many other people tried to convince everyone that the Earth was flat. In 1956, Samuel Shenton set up the Flat Earth Society based on Samuel Rowbotham's work. The Flat Earth Society is still active today.

People travel the world. They go on holiday or travel for business.

With all this evidence it is hard to believe that the Flat Earth Society is still supported today.

If the Earth was flat, what would happen when we came to the edge?

A 'flat' Earth and a spherical Earth

Researching the shape of the Earth, Sun and Moon

Plan a leaflet to show younger children in your school that the Earth, Sun and Moon are spheres. Think about the following questions to help you.

- What evidence can you use?
- Is the evidence reliable?
- Where will you get the information from?
- Can you find any evidence to prove that they are flat?

Check how much you know.
Try the questions on pages 112–113.

Key idea

We know that the Earth and many celestial bodies such as the Sun, planets and moons are spheres.

4 Earth and Space

111

1 Label the diagram below. Use the words in the word box.

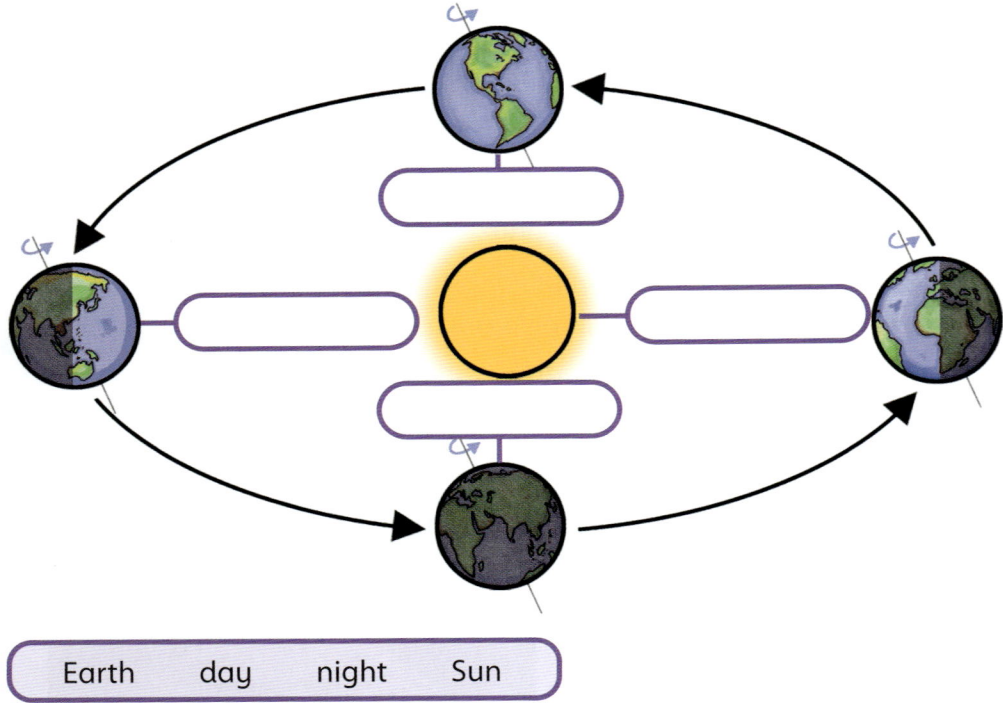

Earth   day   night   Sun

2 Circle the correct word to complete the statement.

    a The time taken for the Earth to spin on its axis is a: day   month   year

    b The time taken for the Earth to revolve around the Sun is a: day   month   year

3 Tick any of the statements that are true about the movement of the Sun and the Earth.

    a The Sun orbits the Earth.

    b The Earth spins on its axis so the Sun appears to move across the sky.

    c The Earth orbits the Sun once every day.

    d The Earth revolves around the Sun once every 365 days.

    e The Earth spins on its axis every day and this gives day and night.

4 Which of the following best describes the movement of the Moon?
Tick the correct answer.

    a The Moon does not move around the Earth, it stays still.

    b The Moon takes a year to orbit the Earth.

    c The Moon takes 27 days (about one month) to orbit the Earth.

■ For more activities, go to Workbook 5 page 112.

5 Mercury, Venus, Earth, Mars and Jupiter are all planets in our solar system. Write down the names of the other three planets. (Hint: they spell 'SUN'!)

_____

_____

_____

6 Look at the diagram below. Draw in and label three straight lines to show the:

- morning shadow
- evening shadow
- midday shadow.

Remember to include the direction AND the length of the shadows.

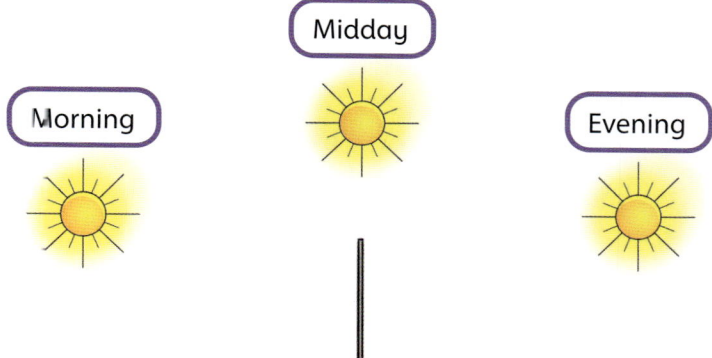

7 What shape is the Earth? Give two pieces of evidence to support this.

_____

_____

_____

_____

■ For more activities, go to Workbook 5 page 113.

In this unit you will:

- explore the force of gravity acting on falling objects
- understand the difference between mass measured in kilograms and weight in newtons
- use units of force, mass and weight
- identify the direction in which forces act
- know and understand the idea of energy in movement
- understand how friction, including air resistance and water resistance, can change the speed objects move
- discover that levers, pulleys and gears allow a smaller force to have a greater effect.

air resistance   energy
force   friction   gravity
inclined plane   lever
machine   mass   multiplier
pulley   water resistance
weight

This rock is being lifted using a simple machine. When have you seen and used simple machines to help you lift, open or close something?

This astronaut is floating in space. Can we do this on Earth?

Why can you jump much higher on the Moon than you can on Earth?

Science fact

Scientists know that objects with large surfaces are held back by air. This is called drag. That is why a snowflake will fall slower than a rain droplet!

■ For more activities, go to Workbook 5 pages 114–115.

Things that go up always come down

In this lesson you will explore gravity and the laws of motion.

Key words

contact force/non-contact force

direction

force

gravity

speed

Think back

Do you know any forces? Make a list.

Scientists have worked for many years to help us understand forces and the world around us. They know that some forces can act on an object without touching it. These are called non-contact forces. Examples include magnetism and gravity. Other forces need to be in contact with an object. Examples include friction, air resistance and pushing or pulling an object.

Discuss any contact and non-contact forces you have seen and used.

The scientist Galileo

The scientist Galileo was born 450 years ago. He investigated why the Moon travelled around the Earth, and was famous for dropping objects from the top of the leaning tower of Pisa in Italy. He dropped metal balls of different weights from the top of the tower and measured how fast they travelled. He discovered that they all travelled at the same speed.

Galileo fired lots of cannon balls from different places. He discovered that the faster the cannon ball travelled the less curved its path was. He thought that if a cannonball travels very fast it will never land on the Earth. It will keep falling. He thought this was how the Moon orbited the Earth but never landed on it.

Do you think Galileo was correct? How can you test this?

Other people believed that a force was pushing the Moon round and round in its orbit.

What are your ideas about how the Moon stays in orbit in space?

■ For more activities, go to Workbook 5 page 116.

Newton and the force of gravity

Isaac Newton was born 380 years ago in England. One day he was sitting under a tree when an apple fell to the ground. Newton realised that the apple was not just falling, but an invisible force was pulling it to the ground. He called this force gravity.

Scientists often find new information that change the ideas of scientists from the past.

Isaac Newton realised that the force of gravity was holding planets in orbit in the solar system. The planets try to fly into space, but they are pulled towards the Sun. Newton also realised that the Moon was being pulled to Earth by gravity. He discovered that the bigger the planet or star, the bigger the force of gravity it has.

What force pulled the apple from the tree to the ground?

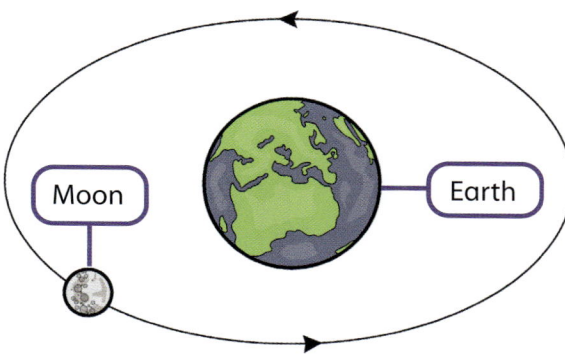

Moon — Earth

The laws of motion

Newton spent many years working out the shapes and sizes of the planets. He worked out rules for gravity and how everything in the universe moves. These are known as the three laws of motion. 'Motion' means movement.

First law: Objects continue doing what they are doing unless other forces speed them up or slow them down.

Second law: Heavier objects need more force to move them.

Third law: Whenever an object pushes another object it gets pushed back in the opposite direction equally hard.

Stretch zone

For the first and second Laws of Motion describe an example of it in action to someone else.

Key idea

Gravity is a force that attracts other objects. That is why unsupported objects will fall to Earth.

5 Forces in Action

117

■ For more activities, go to Workbook 5 page 117.

Mass and weight

In this lesson you will understand the difference between mass measured in kilograms and weight in newtons.

Key words
kilogram (kg)
mass
newton (N)
weight

A newton is a unit of measurement. We sometimes just write N in the same way that we would write kg instead of kilogram.

Isaac Newton investigated gravity for a long time. We now know that gravity pulls you down towards the centre of the Earth. This is true when you are in the air, in water or just standing on land.

Wherever you are on Earth the force of gravity is almost the same.

When you throw a ball up in the air, what happens to it?

When shopkeepers weigh fruit, what unit of measurement do they use?

Most people talk about weight being measured in kilograms. This is incorrect but it is easier for us to think about it in this way. Mass is the amount of matter or particles in an object. It is measured in kilograms or kg for short. Weight is the force of gravity. Scientists measure all forces in newtons.

Investigating weight and mass

On Earth, a mass of 1 kg weighs about 10 N. How can you investigate this?

We use forcemeters to measure the mass and the weight of an object. With special scales we can even measure our mass and weight.

■ For more activities, go to Workbook 5 page 118.

1 Copy the table below in your notebook and add five blank rows.

2 Find five objects. Measure the mass and weight of each object and record the results in your table. One example is given for you.

Object	Mass	Weight
1 litre bottle of water	1 kg	10 N

3 a Are the results you collected reliable?

   b What can you do in your investigation to help you get reliable results?

   c Can you see a pattern in your results?

Remember: 1kg is 10 N.

Astronauts need to understand the difference between mass and weight. The Moon is much smaller than the Earth. It has a much smaller force of gravity. Some other planets are much bigger than the Earth. Their force of gravity is much bigger.

Investigating forces of gravity for planets

Copy the table below and rank the planets in order of their force of gravity.

Planet	Mass compared to Earth	Rank force of gravity
Uranus	14.5	
Jupiter	316	
Mars	11	
Mercury	0.05	
Earth	1	
Saturn	95	
Venus	0.8	
Neptune	17	

Science fact

On larger planets the gravity is so strong a person would weigh much more than they do on Earth. For example, on Jupiter a person who weighs 60 kg on Earth would weigh 140 kg!

Key ideas

- Weight is measured in newtons (N), but we use kilograms (kg) in everyday life.
- Planets with greater mass have a stronger force of gravity.

■ For more activities, go to Workbook 5 page 119.

Investigating gravity, mass and weight

In this lesson you will investigate the relationship between gravity, mass and weight.

Key words
force
mass
weight

Think back

What is the unit of measurement of the force of gravity on Earth?

Why do we say a person has a weight of 60 kg when we mean a mass of 60 kg?

If you are an astronaut and you have a mass of 60 kg on Earth, you weigh 600 newtons (N). When you set off in your rocket and arrive at the Moon you will only weigh 100 N.

Does this mean that during your journey to the Moon you lost mass?

600 N

Earth

100 N

Moon

It takes about two days to travel to the Moon in a spaceship. It is not possible to lose weight so quickly. You cannot lose mass that quickly either. It must be the force of gravity that has changed.

The size of the force of gravity is related to the size of the planet. The greater the mass of an object the greater the gravity is.

If an astronaut has a mass of 120 kg, on Earth they weigh 1200 N. On the Moon they weigh 200 N because the force of gravity is six times less.

Even with a heavy spacesuit the astronaut's weight is much less than on Earth. They can move more easily. The force of gravity is much less and so this is not pulling them to the surface of the Moon.

Is the force of gravity the same everywhere?

Does this mean the Earth is smaller than the Moon? Or is it bigger?

Look at the picture of the astronaut walking on the Moon. Can you explain why they walk on the Moon like this?

■ For more activities, go to Workbook 5 page 120.

Analysing the effect of gravity on weight

You are going to explore how gravity affects weight.

A student has a mass of 40 kg. She wants to find out how much she will weigh on other planets and on the Moon. She researches the gravity on the planets and the Moon. She then calculates her weight. Here are her results.

Planet	Force of gravity per kg	Weight of the student (N)
Mercury	4	160
Venus	9	360
Earth	10	400
Mars	4	160
Jupiter	25	1000
Saturn	9	360
Uranus	8	320
Neptune	11	440
Moon	1.66	80

Remember: The Moon is not a planet.

1 Decide how you are going to show the results. Are you going to use a graph or a chart? What type and why?

2 What are the rules for drawing good graphs and charts?

3 Can you see a pattern in the results? Describe your observations.

4 On what planet does the student weigh the most?

5 What is her mass on every planet?

6 Use the information to write a conclusion describing what the data tells you about mass and weight on other planets.

Stretch zone

Research the atmosphere and the temperature on the surface of one of the planets of the solar system. Give a short talk to the class to share ideas about your planet. Discuss all the planets. Decide which would be the least likely to have life on it and why.

Science fact

On Mercury, an elephant will weigh less than half its weight on Earth. On the Moon, you may be able to lift an elephant!

 Be a scientist

Scientists look for patterns in data and results. This helps them to understand the relationships between the variables.

▶ page 9

Key idea

Gravity is different on the Moon and other planets.

■ For more activities, go to Workbook 5 page 121.

Measuring mass and weight

In this lesson you will use units of force, mass and weight.

Key words

mass

newtons

weight

Think back

How does a forcemeter work? What units are used to measure forces?

Weight in newtons =
mass in kilograms × 10

Very small and very large objects are difficult to measure in kilograms. We use different units to measure them. We measure small objects in grams. Very big objects are measured in metric tonnes.

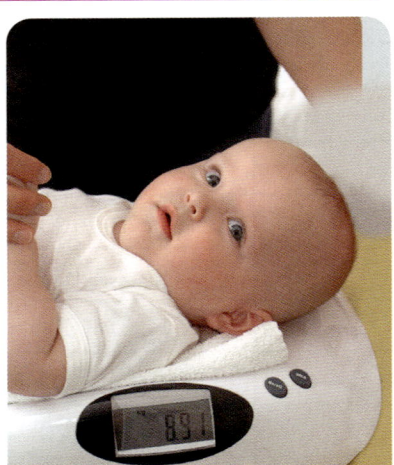

1000 grams = 1 kilogram
1000 kilograms = 1 metric tonne

A baby has a mass of 8.91 kilograms. What is its weight in newtons?

Exploring units of mass

1 What unit do we use to measure our mass?

2 What unit would you use to measure the mass of a grain of rice?

3 Match the pictures with the correct unit of measurement.
Use the word box to help you.

Justify each of your answers.

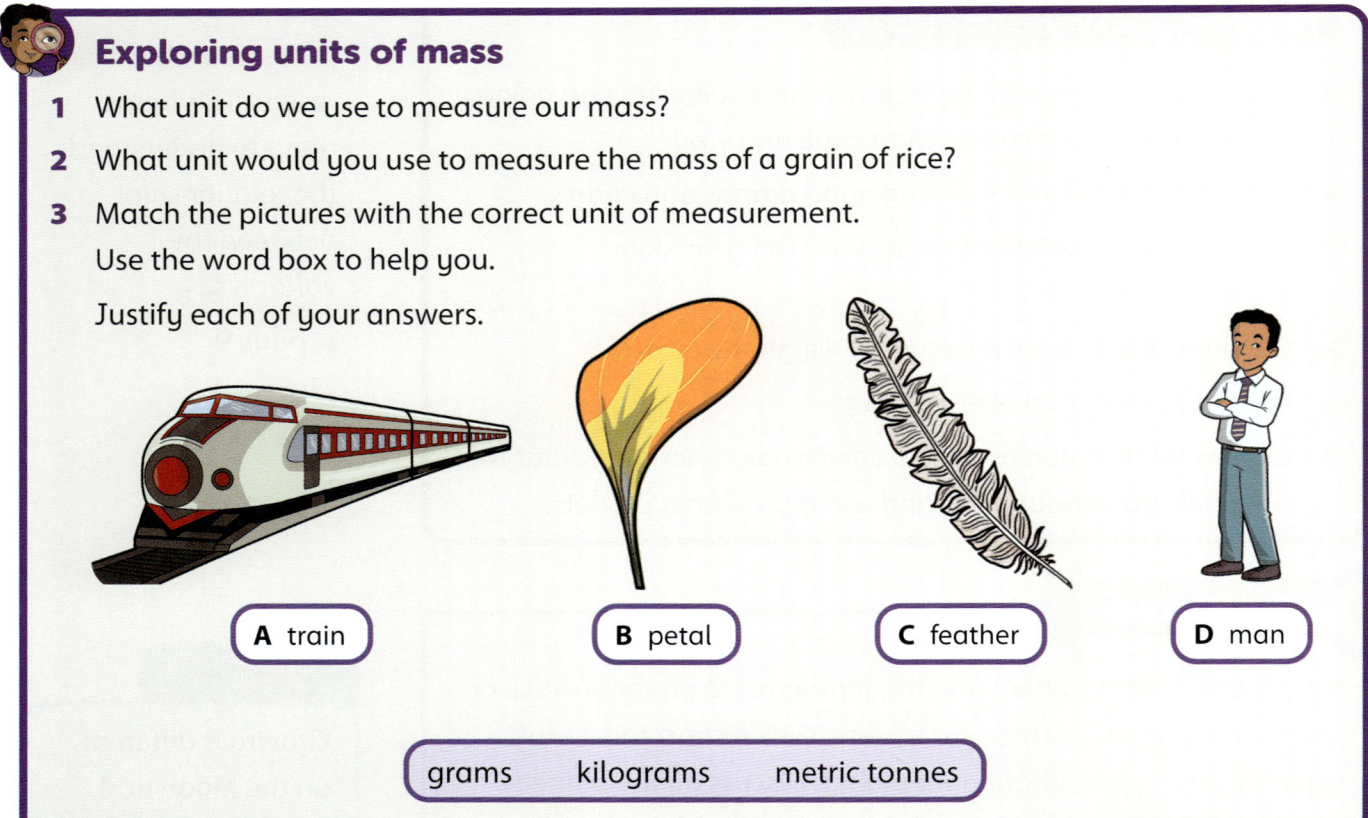

A train B petal C feather D man

grams   kilograms   metric tonnes

■ For more activities, go to Workbook 5 page 122.

Forcemeters are used to measure forces. They contain a spring that is linked to a hook. When the hook is being used to lift or pull something the spring stretches. The greater the force the more the spring will stretch. This gives a bigger reading.

Making a forcemeter

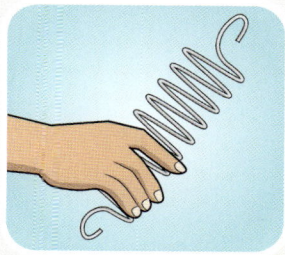

1 Take a spring.

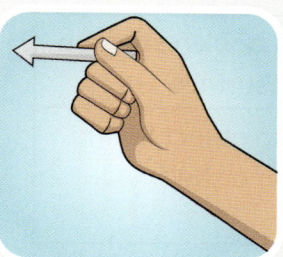

2 Make a cardboard arrow.

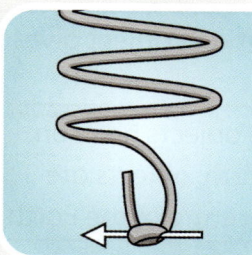

3 Attach the arrow to the bottom coil of the spring using tape.

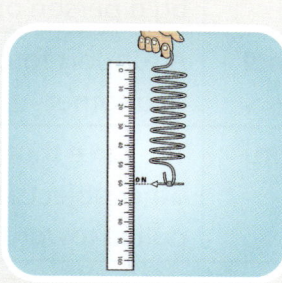

4 Take the spring by the top coil and hold it next to an upright ruler.

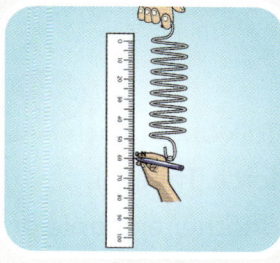

5 Mark where the arrow reaches as zero.

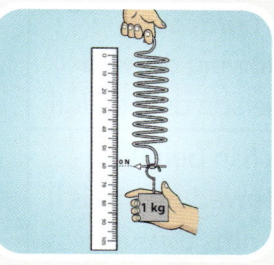

6 Hang a 1 kg mass from the bottom of the spring.

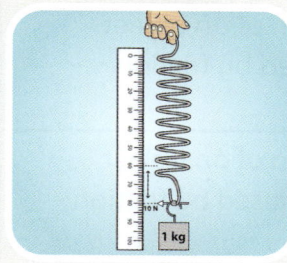

7 Mark this as 10 N on the ruler.

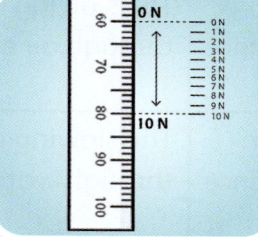

8 Divide the gap between 0 and 10 N into 10 equal sections of 1 N.

9 Use your forcemeter to measure the weights of three objects in the classroom. Record them in your notebook.

10 a How accurate is your forcemeter?

  b How can you alter it so you can weigh objects up to 5 N in weight?

Stretch zone

Design a forcemeter that could lift a person. Decide what you could use for a spring. Could you use more than one spring? Draw your design.

Key ideas

- Mass is the amount of material in an object. It is measured in grams, kilograms or metric tonnes.
- Weight is the force of gravity acting on an object. It is measured in newtons.

■ For more activities, go to Workbook 5 page 123.

Investigating forces

In this lesson you will identify the size and direction of forces.

You have seen and experienced a lot of different forces. Scientists give forces special names.

Key words

direction
force
gravity
upthrust

Name	What it is	Example
Applied force	A force that is used against an object by a person or another object	A person pushing a door closed
Normal force	A support force that one object gives to another	A book resting on a surface
Gravity	The force that large objects have on other objects. On Earth, objects are pulled towards the centre of the Earth	An object falling off a shelf
Upthrust	The upward force liquids have on objects floating in it	Water keeping a boat afloat
Friction	The force created when one surface rubs past another	Car tyres gripping the road
Air resistance	The slowing down of an object through air caused by friction	A parachute slowing down a person as they fall
Water resistance	The slowing down of an object through water caused by friction	A fish being slowed down as it swims through water

Talk about each force. Think of another example of each one.

Whenever an object pushes another object it gets pushed back in the opposite direction equally hard. This is an example of how an object has more than one force acting on it. When a car moves along a road, it has the forces of gravity, normal force, air resistance, tyre friction and the thrust of the engine acting on it. You will learn more about these forces later in this unit.

Pushing a wall!

1 Stand in front of a wall. Push against the wall.

2 What happens? Can you push the wall over?

3 What do you feel when you push against the wall?

Remember: When you push against a solid object, such as a wall, you can feel a force pushing back. This is called an opposite force. Think back to Newton's third law of motion.

If you place an object on weighing scales it bounces up and down for a while. This is because the forces are acting against each other.

■ For more activities, go to Workbook 5 page 124.

The boy in the picture is applying a pulling force to the spring. The spring wants to stay in a coiled shape. He needs to use up energy to uncoil it. The spring pulls back in the opposite direction to try to keep its shape. Elastic bands behave in the same way.

Investigating elastic bands

1 Place an elastic band around the end of your finger on one hand.

2 Place the other end around your finger on the other hand. Carefully pull the elastic band apart. What do you feel?

3 Stop pulling and observe what happens to the elastic band. Does the elastic band behave like the spring and pull back in the opposite direction that you pulled in?

We know that the invisible forces acting on an object are balanced if the object does not change speed or direction. We can show forces using arrows. The arrow points in the direction of the force. The size of the arrow shows the size of the force.

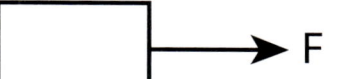

The downward arrow shows the force and direction of gravity on a vase of flowers. There is a second force acting on it. We know this or the vase of flowers would be at the centre of the Earth. The name of the force is normal force.

How would you draw an arrow on the diagram to show normal force?

Key idea

Invisible forces are acting all around us. We can show the strength and direction of these forces using arrows.

Stretch zone

Draw a picture of yourself playing your favourite sport. Add force arrows to show the forces acting on you and any objects you use.

5 Forces in Action

125

■ For more activities, go to Workbook 5 page 125.

Investigating magnetism and floating

In this lesson you will identify magnetic forces and forces acting on objects that float or sink.

Key words
float/sink
magnetism

Floating and sinking

Science fact

An oil tanker weighs 70 000 tonnes. But it still floats.

Objects float if the force they push down with is the same as the water pushing back. The object is pushing down because of the force of gravity. The pushing back is the upthrust from the water.

The forces are balanced so the boat floats. If the upthrust is too small, the boat sinks. Spreading out the weight of an object can help it to float. This is why a flat metal lid floats but a lump of metal of the same mass does not.

List the forces that act on a floating object.

Can you sink an object by increasing its weight?

1 Copy the table into your notebook. Use it to record your results.

Size of lid (cm)	Number of pins needed to sink it
small	
medium	

2 Is there a pattern between the size of the lid and the number of pins needed to sink it?

3 Write a concluding sentence about your investigation.

How does your investigation explain why heavy metal ships float but pins do not?

■ For more activities, go to Workbook 5 page 126.

Have you ever wondered why some things float and some do not?

Floating and sinking

You are going to investigate some objects your teacher gives you.

1 Choose three objects and see which ones float and which ones do not.

2 Copy the table into your notebook and record your results.

Object	Floats	Sinks
stone		yes

3 Which objects sink and which objects float? Can you see a pattern?

Imagine trying to push a plastic ball under water.
What does it feel like?

You are pushing down on the water. The water is pushing back.

Magnetism

The invisible force of magnetism attracts the object to the magnet.

You cannot see the force of magnetism, but you can see the effects.

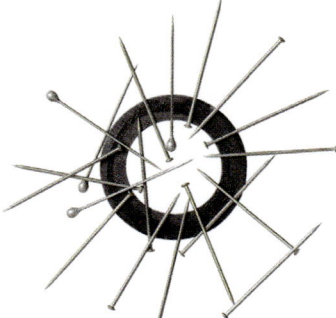

If you hold a magnet close to a magnetic material what can you feel?

Key ideas

- Upthrust and gravity act on objects in water in opposite directions.
- Magnetism is also a force that acts on some objects.

■ For more activities, go to Workbook 5 page 127.

Balanced and unbalanced forces

In this lesson you will explore the idea of balanced and unbalanced forces.

Key words

balanced/
  unbalanced
direction
force
friction
speed

Think back

How can forces change the shape of an object?

What other effects of forces can you remember?

When the forces on an object change, this has an effect on the object.

When you squeeze a soft ball, you are applying a force. The ball pushes back against the push from the squeeze. If the force from the squeeze is bigger, the ball will change shape.

For an object to move, the push force has to be more than any forces holding the object in place. One force to overcome is called friction. Friction is a force that is made when one surface rubs against another. It slows down a moving object. You will study more about friction later.

 **Exploring forces**

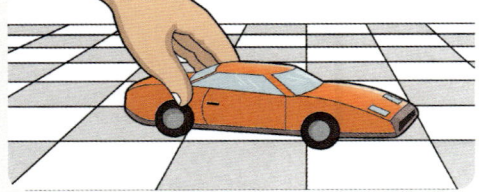

1. Place a toy car on a flat surface. Observe what happens to the car.

2. If you push the car a little, what happens?

3. Push the car more to the left. What do you observe?

4. Push the car more to the right. What do you observe?

We can change the direction of an object by changing the size and position of the force. This can be very useful when driving a car.

When have you changed the direction of an object? Think about sports you have played or things you have pushed or pulled.

What forces are needed for these cars to speed up?

128

■ For more activities, go to Workbook 5 page 128.

When the forces are the same, we call them balanced. This means nothing happens.

When you observed your toy car at the beginning of your investigation it did nothing. This means the forces were balanced.

When you pushed your car, it moved. This means the forces were now no longer balanced and something happened. The car moved!

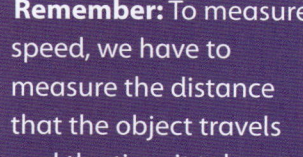

How can you measure whether the change in force changes the speed of an object?

How do we measure speed?

Remember: To measure speed, we have to measure the distance that the object travels and the time it takes.

Measuring the speed of a toy car

You are going to measure how the angle of a ramp affects the speed of a toy car.

1 Use an angle measurer to set up a ramp using a piece of wood and a pile of books. Set the ramp at a 20-degree angle.
2 Measure from the top of the ramp and draw a line on the floor or desk so the car will travel exactly 1 metre.
3 Place the toy car at the top of the ramp. Let go of the car and time how long it takes to travel 1 metre.
4 Repeat the investigation using all of the angles shown in the table.
5 Copy the table below into your notebook and record your results.

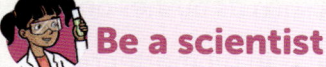 **Be a scientist**

Scientists will repeat an investigation to make sure they can trust the result. They obtain an average reading for each run.

▶ page 10

Angle of the ramp (degrees)	Time taken to travel 1 metre (s)	Speed (m/s)
20	6	0.16
30		
40		
50		
60		

6 Can you notice any pattern in your results?

How else can you speed up the car?

Stretch zone

Plan an investigation to find out whether the surface has an effect on the speed of the car. How will you make this a fair test?

Key idea

Forces can change the direction and speed of an object.

5 Forces in Action

129

 For more activities, go to Workbook 5 page 129.

Energy transfers

In this lesson you discover that energy can be transferred but never created or destroyed.

Key words

create/destroy
energy
kinetic energy
transfer

Think back

Discuss any forms of energy that you know about or have heard of. Make a list in your notebook.

Add more to the list as you learn about them.

There are many different forms of energy. Electrical and heat (or thermal) energy are two types. Our food contains chemical energy. Our body converts this chemical energy into many other kinds of energy. For example, it is changed to kinetic energy when we move.

Kinetic energy is a scientific term that means movement energy.

Forces such as pushes and pulls must use energy or nothing will happen.

Energy is in all matter and is also in sound, light and heat. This energy cannot be created or destroyed. It is never used up but it can be transferred from one form of energy to another. For example when a fuel burns, the chemical energy is changed to heat and light energy.

Where do you get your energy from?

When you pushed the toy car in the investigation on page 128, where did the energy come from?

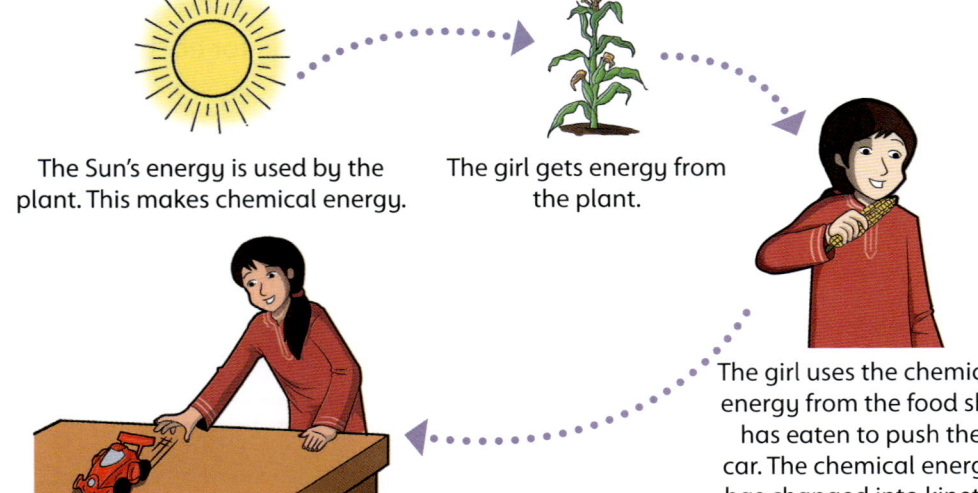

The Sun's energy is used by the plant. This makes chemical energy.

The girl gets energy from the plant.

The girl uses the chemical energy from the food she has eaten to push the car. The chemical energy has changed into kinetic energy.

What are the energy transfers when a computer or a TV is working? Talk about why the back of a computer or TV can get very hot when it is working. What does this tell you about energy transfer?

At every stage in an energy transfer some energy is lost to the surroundings. This is often as heat or sound.

■ For more activities, go to Workbook 5 page 130.

Once a toy car is moving it will continue at the same speed and in the same direction. If another force is applied, it may change speed or stop altogether.

Energy is measured in joules. To pick a book up you will need about 1 joule of energy. To pick more books up you will need more joules of energy. If you want to move the books to another room, you need even more joules of energy.

How many joules of energy will you need to pick up:
a) 10 books and
b) 20 books?

A cyclist has to work hard to make a bicycle go fast. The amount of work this cyclist does depends on:

- the distance she travels
- the mass of what she is moving. This is the bicycle and herself and the force of gravity (10 N/kg). We can change the mass to force by multiplying by 10.

The more force you have to use to move an object the more work you will be doing. That is why moving heavy objects a long way takes more work than moving a light object a small distance.

Stretch zone

Plan a survey of your local area to find examples of energy being used to make things move, speed up, slow down, change direction or change shape. Make an information leaflet with the title 'Energy and forces around me'.

Key ideas

- Energy is in all matter. It can be transferred but never created or destroyed.
- Energy is used when forces are applied.

■ For more activities, go to Workbook 5 page 131.

Investigating friction

In this lesson you will explore the force of friction.

Key word
friction

Think back

The direction of the arrows shows the direction of the force.

Which force happens when one surface rubs against another?

List three examples to share with the class.

There are other forces acting on the car. The engine is pushing the car forward. Also, when two surfaces touch each other they slow each other down. This is called friction.

How would you draw arrows on the picture to show the forces on this parked car?

Friction gives us grip on things such as shoes and car tyres. The brakes on a bicycle and a car also rely on friction. Sometimes we do not want a lot of grip. If people are ice skating or skiing they want to go faster without being slowed down.

Rough surfaces give a lot of friction

Smooth surfaces reduce friction

Machine parts are helped to move without friction by adding oil.

Why is oil added to machines?

■ For more activities, go to Workbook 5 page 132.

Investigating surfaces

1 Set up a ramp that has an angle of 30 degrees.

2 Cover the ramp with aluminium foil. Place a car at the top of the ramp.

3 Let the car go and time how long it takes to reach the bottom of the ramp.

4 Investigate placing different surfaces onto your ramp to see if it slows down or speeds up the car. Predict what you think will happen each time.

5 Use a table like the one below to record your results.

Surface	Time taken for the car to roll down the ramp (seconds)				
	Predicted	Run 1	Run 2	Run 3	Average (mean)
aluminium foil					

6 Write a report of your investigation. Include a description of your method, the variables in the investigation, your predictions and results.

Moving objects

It is more difficult to draw force arrows on things that move. We have to work out which force is having the biggest effect. If the car is driving along the road, the push from the engine must be greater than the force of friction.

We draw a thick arrow (⟶) to show a bigger force.

A thin arrow (⟶) shows a weaker force.

Stretch zone

Think about how your shoes create friction between your shoe and the floor. Make a small poster showing two examples of footwear that help people to slide as part of sport and two examples of footwear designed to stop people from slipping when doing sport.

What happens if the force of friction increases?

Use your learning to discuss how to draw arrows on the diagram of the car opposite when it is moving forward.

Key ideas

- Friction is a force made when two surfaces rub together.
- Rough surfaces create more friction than smooth surfaces.

5 Forces in Action

133

■ For more activities, go to Workbook 5 page 133.

Friction and air resistance

In this lesson you will discover how friction and air resistance slow things down.

Think back

List all the forces that you have learned about so far.

Can you remember how friction affected your toy car?

Friction and energy

How does friction help the Formula 1 driver?

Friction can be very useful. It helps cars and buses to slow down and stop. This is how brakes work. If a large surface area is touching, then friction will be greater. This is why racing cars have wide tyres. There is more of each tyre touching the road, so it grips more.

Investigating friction and energy

1 Rub two of your fingers together quickly. What do you feel?

2 Now rub your hands together quickly. What do you feel?

Notice how your hands became hotter. More skin surface rubbed together and so more friction was made.

Air resistance

As objects move through the air they are held back. Scientists call this air resistance or drag. The amount of air resistance depends on the size or surface area. Shape can also affect the amount of air resistance.

A small object cuts through the air better than a large object and so air resistance is lower.

■ For more activities, go to Workbook 5 page 134.

Investigate air resistance with paper

1 Drop a piece of flat paper and observe how quickly it travels to the ground.

2 What forces are acting on the paper?

3 Now scrunch the paper into a ball. What do you observe when you drop the scrunched paper?

4 Measure the height you drop the paper from and keep it the same. Time how long it takes to drop to the ground.

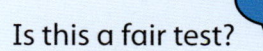 Is this a fair test?

5 Record your results in a copy of the table below in your notebook.

What piece of equipment will you use to measure the time taken?

Paper type	Time taken to fall (seconds): try 1	Time taken to fall (seconds): try 2	Time taken to fall (seconds): try 3
flat			
scrunched			

6 a What do you notice about the time it takes for both pieces of paper to fall?

b Do they take the same amount of time to fall?

What two things affect the amount of air resistance the most?

The flat piece of paper has the bigger surface area. This means that it is being affected more by air resistance. The scrunched-up paper has a smaller surface area. This means it is less affected by the force of air resistance. Air resistance is an example of friction. The object is rubbing against particles in the air.

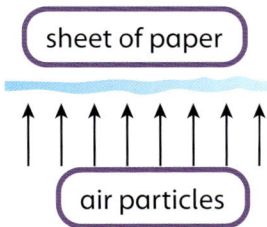

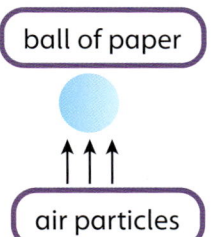

 Stretch zone

Find some photographs on the internet of racing cars, downhill skiers and professional cyclists. Use your knowledge of air resistance to explain how each of them reduce air resistance to go faster.

Key idea

Friction and air resistance slow things down.

5 Forces in Action

135

■ For more activities, go to Workbook 5 page 135.

Friction and water resistance

In this lesson you will identify the effects of water resistance.

Think back

What forces are acting on the parachutist? How is the parachutist using air resistance?

Key words

air resistance
streamline
water resistance

Science fact

In 2012 Felix Baumgartner jumped out of a balloon 39 km above the Earth. It took more than four minutes for him to safely land.

When people use a parachute to land back on Earth it is called parachuting or sky diving.

Parachutes use the force of air resistance. The parachute is designed to increase air resistance. The large surface area of the parachute hits many more air particles than a person's body. This helps the parachutist to fall very slowly.

It depends on the distance jumped, but if there was no air a parachutist could hit the ground at more than 1000 kilometres per hour (km/h) even with a parachute.

Water resistance

The particles in air that slow down a parachute are far apart. Particles in water are much closer together. This causes water resistance.

Animals and human-made objects are streamlined

The shape of an object can help it to move through water. Just like in air a large surface will slow objects that are passing through water. A narrow shape will help an object to cut through water. Scientists call this streamlining.

Do you think an object falling through water will be slowed down more than when it falls through air? Why?

■ For more activities, go to Workbook 5 page 136.

Investigating water resistance

1 Cut the narrow neck off a tall plastic drinks bottle.

2 Place the bottle on a tray and fill the bottle to the top with water.

3 Use same-size pieces of modelling clay to make the shapes shown here. They need to be able to fit into the bottle. Tie a long piece of cotton to the end of each shape so you can pull them back out of the water.

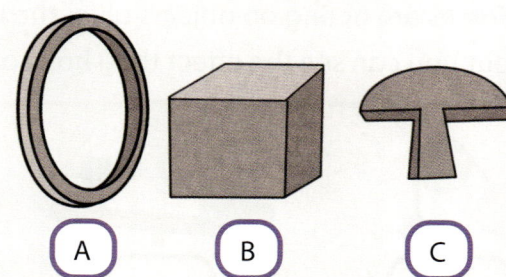

4 Predict which of the shapes will sink to the bottom of the bottle in the least amount of time. Write your prediction in your notebook.

5 Take shape **A** and hold it so it just touches the surface of the water.

6 Let go and time how long it takes to sink to the bottom of the water. Complete a table like the one below.

7 Repeat the investigation with **A** three times to find an average time.

8 Time and record the time it takes shapes **B** and **C** to sink.

Shape	Time for the shape to sink to the bottom (seconds)			
	Try 1	Try 2	Try 3	Average (mean)
A				

Discuss in your group if there is a pattern in the results that you have collected.

9 Which shape took the least time to sink? Which one took the most time to sink?

10 Can you explain how water resistance affected your results?

11 In your notebook, write a conclusion about your results. Include the word 'streamlining'. Add force diagrams for your shapes.

Be a scientist

Scientists present their data in a way that shows how their investigations support their results.

▶ page 11

Key ideas

- Water slows objects down that are trying to move through it. This is called water resistance.
- Streamlined objects pass through water more easily.

■ For more activities, go to Workbook 5 page 137.

5 Forces in Action

Investigating simple machines

In this lesson you will discover that some machines allow a smaller force to have a greater effect.

Think back

Forces are acting on objects all of the time. You cannot see forces but you can see the effect they have on objects.

Key words

energy
inclined plane
lever
machine
multiplier
pulley

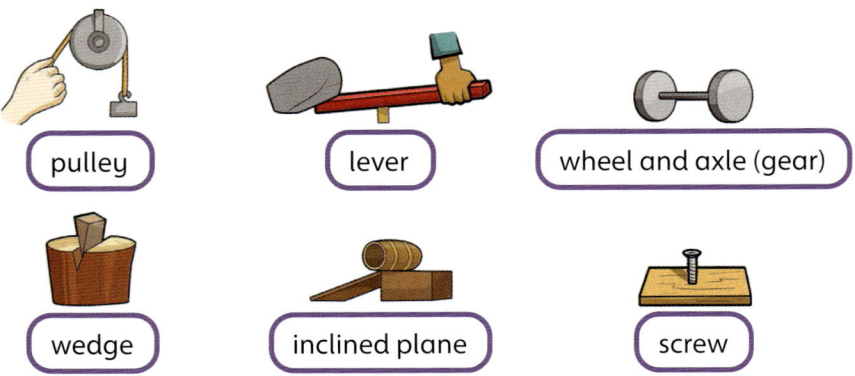

pulley

lever

wheel and axle (gear)

wedge

inclined plane

screw

Do you recognise any of the objects in the pictures?

Do you know how any are used?

These are all simple machines. There are six simple machines that we use to help us to do work. They are called force multipliers because they take a small force and make it bigger. For example, gripping with pliers instead of just your hand makes the gripping force bigger. You will explore pulleys, inclined planes and levers.

Pulley

A pulley is a simple machine that is used to lift objects to a higher level. Forces are still needed to move from one level to the higher level, but less energy is needed.

The force used to lift the object is known as the effort. This is shown by an arrow in the direction of pull. The object being lifted is the load. This has a down arrow because the force of gravity is pulling downwards, giving it weight.

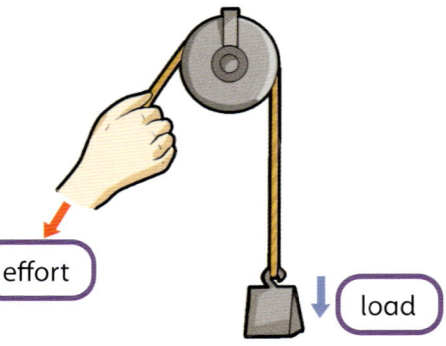

effort

load

Simple pulley system

Investigating a pulley

Your teacher will demonstrate how the pulley system works.

1 Pick up the load without using the pulley and describe what it feels like.

2 Now use the pulley to pick up the load. Does this make it easier?

3 Draw a diagram of the pulley system. Label the load and effort and add force arrows to explain how it works.

138

Inclined plane

An inclined plane is used to move an object or a person from a lower level to a higher one. It is a flat surface with one end higher than the other.

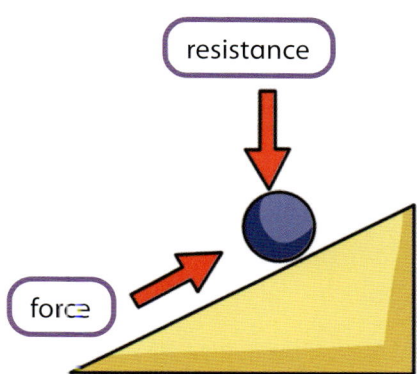

resistance

force

An escalator

Have you seen or used an escalator?

Which simple machine is an escalator?

Can you see how this machine makes work easier?

Does an inclined plane use less energy?

You will need a forcemeter, books and weights.

1 Attach the forcemeter to the weight using the hook.

2 Hold a ruler vertical to the desk.

3 Lift the weight to a height of 30 cm and record the measurement on the forcemeter.

4 Repeat this to make sure that the results are reliable.

5 Make a stack of books so that they are at the same height of 30 cm. Lean another book up to the pile of books to make an inclined plane. Place the weight at the bottom of the inclined plane.

6 Pull the weight up the inclined plane to the top. Record the measurement on the forcemeter.

7 Repeat the investigation until you have reliable results.

8 Does the inclined plane make the work easier? Explain how.

Warning! Be careful when using weights. Do not drop them on your feet or hands. Always work over a desk or table.

Be a scientist

Scientists repeat tests until they have at least three results that are almost the same. If one result is very different from the others, they will probably ignore it as a mistake.

▶ page 10

Stretch zone

Research how a wheel and axle, screw, and wedge are used. For each one, draw a diagram and describe an example of it being used.

Key idea

Simple machines are used to do jobs using less energy.

■ For more activities, go to Workbook 5 page 139.

Using levers as a force multiplier

In this lesson you will discover that levers allow a smaller force to have a greater effect.

Think back

A force multiplier means less effort is needed to carry out work.

load   fulcrum   effort

What can you see in the photograph?

What is this used for?

A seesaw is an example of a lever. This is a simple machine that is used to lift heavy objects using less energy.

The scissors and the bottle opener are both acting as simple machines. They are multiplying the force of the person's hands. If you look carefully, you will see that both are levers.

What have these two objects got in common?

How are they being used?

Using levers

Your teacher will show you a board with a pin in it.

1   Try to remove the pin. Is it difficult?

2   Now try using a claw hammer. This is a lever.

Warning! Be careful when trying to remove the pin. Discuss why this is important.

Is the claw hammer a force multiplier? Discuss why this is.

3   Is less effort needed to remove the pin using the claw hammer?

Science fact

Massive cranes used in construction are simple levers.

140

■ For more activities, go to Workbook 5 page 140

Investigating levers

You are going to investigate if levers reduce the force needed to lift an object.

Your teacher will give you a book, an elastic band, string and a ruler.

1   Tie the string around the middle of the book and attach the elastic band.

2   Lift the book 5 cm up from the surface of the desk. Measure the extension in the elastic band. Record the measurement. Make sure your results are reliable.

3   Now place the book on the edge of the desk. Push a ruler under the book until it is about half way under.

4   Attach the elastic band to the end of the ruler. Pull the elastic band down. This will result in the ruler being used as a lever.

5 cm

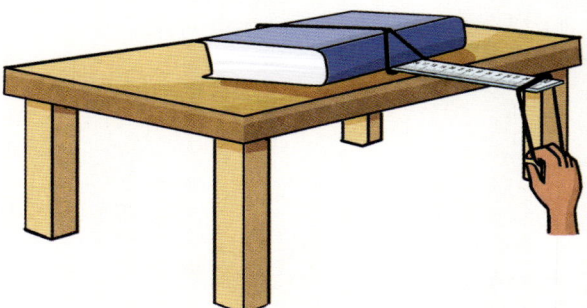

5   Raise the book 5 cm up from the surface of the desk. Measure the extension in the elastic band. Record your measurements.

6   Analyse your results and make your conclusions. If the elastic band extended less, then less force was needed to raise the book.

Does the ruler act like a force multiplier?

Discuss why this is.

When using a lever, the effort you need to move a load is reduced.

Stretch zone

Record all of the uses of simple machines that you see or use for the rest of the day.

Check how much you know.
Try the questions on pages 142–143.

Key idea

Levers are used in everyday life to make work easier.

■ For more activities, go to Workbook 5 page 141.

What have I learned about forces in action?

For questions 1 and 2 circle the correct answer.

1 The force that attracts objects to the centre of the Earth is:

electricity   friction   gravity   magnetism

2 The unit of measurement for force is:

kilogram   newton   seconds   volt

3 Complete the sentences by filling in the missing words. The words are in the word box.

A force can change the **s**_____ and **d**_____ of an object.

A force can make an object **s**_____ to move, **s**_____ down or **s**_____.

> direction   slow   speed   start   stop

4 An oil tanker with a mass of 70 000 tonnes weighs 70 000 000 N! What force

keeps the ship afloat? _____

5 a Label the simple machine below. Use the words in the word box.

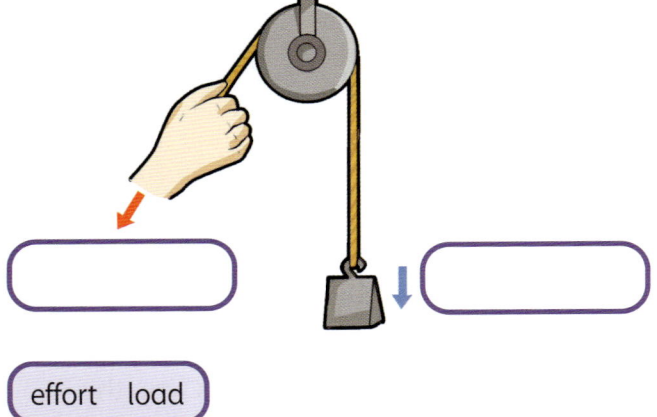

> effort   load

b Name this simple machine. _____

c Explain the term force muliplier.

_____

6 Draw in the force arrows to show the forces acting on the moving car below.

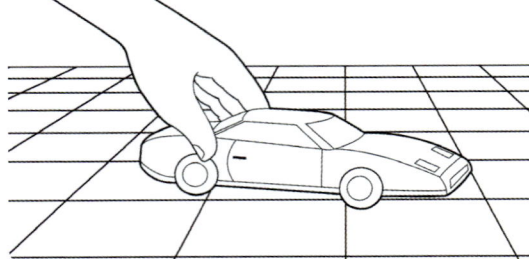

■ For more activities, go to Workbook 5 page 142.

7 Complete the energy transfers below by writing in the missing words from the word box.

> heat   light   sound   movement

a Electrical energy in a TV is transferred to heat, _____ and _____.

b Chemical energy in coal is transferred to _____ and _____.

c Electrical energy in a drill is transferred to _____, _____ and heat.

8 Use the pictures below to answer the questions about an investigation.

A   B   C

a Name the force that slows the parachutes down as they fall. _____

b A group of students carried out an investigation by dropping the parachutes. They forgot to label the parachutes. They also forgot to work out the average (mean) times. Work out the mean times and add them to the table below. Analyse the results and then decide which parachute is which. Put the correct letter into the first column in the table.

Parachute	Time taken for the parachutes to fall (seconds)			
	Try 1	**Try 2**	**Try 3**	**Average (mean)**
	4	5	6	
	2	2	4	
	7	6	8	

c What is the independent variable for this investigation? _____

d What is the dependent variable for this investigation? _____

e Write down two variables that the students had to control to help to make this a fair test.

_____ and _____

■ For more activities, go to Workbook 5 page 143.

Glossary

adolescent

air resistance

amphibian

axis

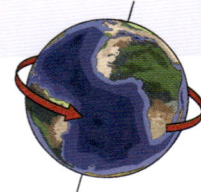

baby

bird

chrysalis

day

dissolve

Earth

energy

feeding

fertilisation

force

friction

fruit

germination

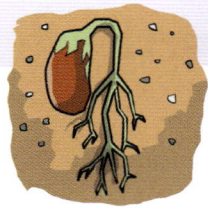

gravity

growth

inclined plane

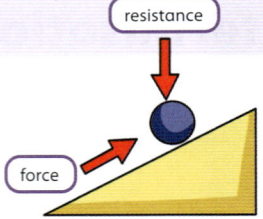

insect

insoluble

irreversible

larva

lever

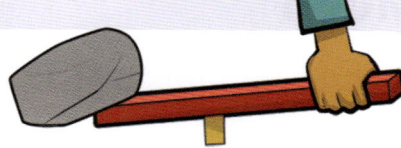

life cycle

living

machine

mammal

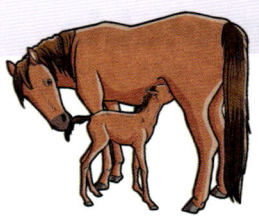

mass

mixture

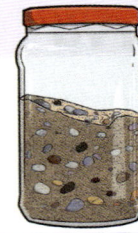

Moon

movement

multiplier

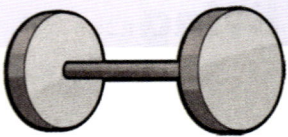

night

orbit

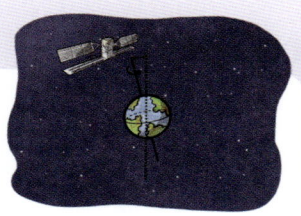

planet

pollination

property

pulley

reaction

reproduction

reversible

rotate

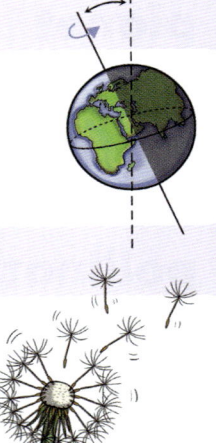

seed dispersal

separate

shadow

solar system

soluble

solute

solution

sphere

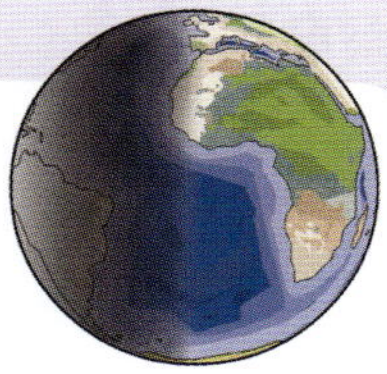

star

Sun

tadpole

warmth

water

water resistance

weight

year